REALISM AND REGIONALISM

(1860–1910)

Jerry Phillips, Ph.D.
General Editor to First Edition

Department of English
University of Connecticut, Storrs

Michael Anesko, Ph.D.
Adviser and Contributor

Director, Honors Program in English
Pennsylvania State University

Roger Lathbury, Ph.D.
Karen Meyers, Ph.D.
Principal Authors

∎ ∎ ∎ ∎

CHELSEA HOUSE
PUBLISHERS
An imprint of Infobase Publishing

Realism and Regionalism (1860–1910)

Copyright © 2010, 2006 by DWJ BOOKS LLC

DEVELOPED AND PRODUCED FOR CHELSEA HOUSE BY DWJ BOOKS LLC

Dedication
To Rachel

Chelsea House
An imprint of Infobase Publishing
132 West 31st Street
New York NY 10001

Library of Congress Cataloging-in-Publication Data

Lathbury, Roger.
    Realism and regionalism : 1860-1910 / Jerry Phillips, general editor; Michael Anesko, adviser and contributor; Roger Lathbury, Karen Meyers, principal authors.—2nd ed.
        p. cm. — (Backgrounds to American literature)
    Includes bibliographical references and index.

ISBN 978-1-60413-487-2 (hardcover: alk. paper)

    1. American literature—19th century—History and criticism. 2. American literature—20th century—History and criticism. 3. Realism in literature. 4. Regionalism in literature. I. Phillips, Jerry (Jerry R.) II. Anesko, Michael. III. Meyers, Karen, 1948- IV. Title. V. Series.
    PS2I7.R4L38 2010
    810.9'12—dc22   2009029631

Chelsea House books are available at special discounts when purchased in bulk quantities for businesses, associations, institutions, or sales promotions. Please call our Special Sales Department in New York at (212) 967-8800 or (800) 322-8755.

You can find Chelsea House on the World Wide Web at http://www.chelseahouse.com

Text design by DWJ BOOKS LLC
Cover printed by Bang Printing, Brainerd, MN
Book printed and bound by Bang Printing, Brainerd, MN
Date printed: April 2010
Printed in the United States of America

Acknowledgments
pp. 5, 25, 45, 49, 101: Library of Congress, Prints and Photographs Division
pp. 23, 39, 65, 69: Courtesy of Roger Lathbury
p. 35 N.Y. Public Library Picture Collection
p. 71: From *How the Other Half Lives, Studies among the Tenements of New York* (1890),
Charles Scribner's Sons
p. 89: AP Photo, Lee Mariner
p. 91: National Portrait Gallery, Smithsonian Institution/Art Resource, New York

10 9 8 7 6 5 4 3 2 1

This book is printed on acid-free paper.

All links and Web addresses were checked and verified to be correct at the time of publication. Because of the dynamic nature of the Web, some addresses and links may have changed since publication and may no longer be valid.

Contents

Preface

▪ ▪

The five volumes of *Backgrounds to American Literature* explore 500 years of American literature by looking at the times during which the literature developed. Through a period's historical antecedents and characteristics—political, cultural, religious, economic, and social—each chapter covers a specific period, theme, or genre.

In this new edition of the series, a final chapter looks at the period through another lens—through the eyes of enslaved peoples. In addition to these seven chapters, readers will find a useful timeline of drama and theatrical history, poetry and prose, and history; a glossary of terms (also identified by throughout the text); a biographical glossary; suggestions for further reading; and an index. By helping readers explore literature in the context of human history, the editors hope to encourage readers to further explore the literary world.

1. Sectionalism, Industrialism, and Literary Regionalism

In 1858, Abraham Lincoln had warned his countrymen "a house divided against itself cannot stand." Events in the dark winter of 1860–61 would prove him correct. After Lincoln's minority election to the presidency, South Carolina voted to secede from the Union in December 1860; six other states of the Deep South quickly followed suit. When Confederate troops successfully attacked Fort Sumter in Charleston harbor on April 12, 1861, Virginia, Arkansas, Tennessee, and North Carolina elected to join their fellows in defense of slavery and the sovereign principle of states' rights.

Historical Overview

While an older generation of historians tended to view the Civil War as the watershed of modern American nationalism (Charles Beard, for example, called it "the second American Revolution"), more recent HISTORIOGRAPHY suggests that the real factors that determined the future of the nation were the facts that the country was still badly fragmented after the war and that Congress did little to address this and other problems. Even though the language of the Constitution itself was amended to affirm an expanded—that is, colorblind—definition of individual rights and liberties, meaningful

Camp of Captain John Huff

This photograph was taken in July of 1865 in Gettysburg, Pennsylvania, by William Morris Smith. A peaceful moment on the site of one of the bloodiest battles of the Civil War, the picture was taken at the rear of the camp. The Battle of Gettysburg took place about two years earlier on July 1–3, 1863.

implementation of that vision for African Americans would have to wait for almost another century.

At the same time, however, the war did unleash a range of social and economic forces that, eventually, would radically transform American life. The Pacific Railroad Act of 1862 set aside vast tracts of public land in the West to finance the construction of a transcontinental railroad; the Homestead Act of 1862 enabled yeoman farmers to have cheaper access to government-held land; and the Morrill Act of 1862 established Federal support for agricultural (land-grant) colleges.

Mobilization for war on such an unprecedented scale also had unforeseen effects on American life. The need to achieve organizational efficiency in both military and civilian branches of government gave rise to an almost wholly new group of managers, who were able to transfer their increasingly professional skills to the business world after the war. One simple but suggestive example illustrates this point. Keeping thousands of men in uniforms required an entirely new approach to apparel manufacturing. At the start of the war, when almost all of the troops came from volunteer contingents of various state militias, mothers, wives, and daughters would have sewed

■ ■ LAND-GRANT COLLEGES ■ ■
The Morrill Act of 1862 provided grants of land to allow for the establishment of colleges. These so-called "land-grant" colleges were originally designed to teach agriculture, military tactics, mechanical arts, and classical studies to working-class individuals who could not afford a university education. The idea was to provide an affordable, practical education to people who wanted to work in agriculture and industry. A second Morrill Act (1890) provided some additional funding for land-grant colleges, but it did not allow money to be spent on colleges that discriminated on the basis of race. In the South where segregation was practiced, the 1890 Morrill Act provided funds for separate black colleges. There is at least one land-grant college in every U.S. state.

The Morrill Act is named after Justin Smith Morrill, a congressman from Vermont, but the idea of a land-grant system was first championed by Jonathan Baldwin Turner. His 1850 paper, "Plan for a State University for the Industrial Classes" outlined many characteristics that have come to be associated with land-grant colleges, such as agricultural research.

individual uniforms at home. Before long, however, the need for additional soldiers made the draft inevitable. The unprecedented demand for huge numbers of identical trousers, jackets, boots, and other mainstays of military regimentation sparked the rapid modernization of the clothing industry by introducing "standard" apparel sizes. The federal government was the first consumer to make its purchases off the rack. These new concepts of scale, efficiency, and organizational complexity would eventually make possible what one influential historian referred to as "the incorporation of America." It is, indeed, the way we live now.

Literary Movements

Politically, the so-called "Radical Republicans" (northern abolitionists led by Senator Charles Sumner of Massachusetts) largely failed in their efforts to secure equal rights for the freed slaves. The difficulty of translating the high-minded idealism of greater New England into effective public policy also illuminates a crucial moment in the nation's intellectual history. As the novelist Henry James (1843–1916) had occasion to observe in 1879, "the Civil War marks an era in the history of the American mind. It introduced into the national consciousness a certain sense of proportion and relation, of the world being a more complicated place than it had hitherto seemed, the future more treacherous, success more difficult. At the rate at which things are going, it is obvious that good Americans will be more numerous than ever; but the good American, in the days to come, will be a more critical person than his complacent and confident grandfather. He has eaten of the tree of knowledge."

We can confirm the relevance of James's conclusion from other types of evidence. By the time that Lee surrendered at Appomattox Court House, his army's ranks were severely depleted, and the same was true for the roll call of American authorship. Washington Irving had died in 1859; Henry David Thoreau in 1862; Nathaniel Hawthorne in 1864. The utter collapse of his literary reputation after the publication of *The Confidence-Man; His Masquerade* (1857) sent Herman Melville into a kind of internal exile and virtual retirement at the New York Customs House. *The Conduct of Life*, arguably Ralph Waldo Emerson's last important book, appeared in 1860. With their passing, the nation looked to new literary voices whose accents were not always so comforting. The cultural supremacy of New England, so long taken for granted, was now open to challenge.

A typical scene from John W. DeForest's *Miss Ravenel's Conversion from Secession to Loyalty* (1867), one of the earliest novels to tackle the subject of the war, neatly serves as a symbol for the impending transition of cultural authority. In a letter home, the book's hero (a Union officer) describes a battlefield incident with almost bemused detachment. Having just finished breakfast, he lies back to smoke and hears a bullet that whistles so unusually low as to attract his attention. The slug strikes with a loud smash in a tree about twenty feet from him. Another man lying on his back reading a newspaper starts as the bullet passes. Other members of the company abandon their card game and go to look for it. "The man who was reading remained perfectly still," DeForest writes,

> his eyes fixed on the paper with a steadiness which I thought curious. . . . They went to him, . . . and found him perfectly dead. The ball had struck him under the chin, traversed the neck, and cut the spinal column where it joins the brain, making a fearful hole through which the blood had already soaked his great-coat. It was this man's head, and not the tree, which had been struck with such a report. There he lay, still holding the New York Independent, with his eyes fixed on a sermon by Henry Ward Beecher.

Although Beecher's sermon probably would have affirmed the beliefs of evangelical Protestantism—especially the idea that God favored the Union cause—DeForest's prose works to undercut the idea that nature is a reflection of the goodness of God. The nameless (and presumably devout) soldier is struck down by a stray shot, an act of random and arbitrary violence; his more profane card-playing comrades survive; the author describes the whole scene with clinical objectivity. In almost every respect, *Miss Ravenel's Conversion* displays the hallmarks of LITERARY REALISM. While the transcendentalists believed in certain moral absolutes—such as self-reliance—realists were skeptical and tended to present such absolutes ironically. Simultaneously, DeForest and other realists focus their attention on the here and now, intent on describing things literally as they see them and know them to be, instead of treating them as symbols of a "higher" realm of spiritual values as the transcendentalists might have.

DeForest was also the first critic to go in search of "The Great American Novel," a phrase he coined in 1868. With his instinctive preference for realism, DeForest dismissed almost all earlier American writing as romantically provincial: Irving was more interested in Europe than his native land; Cooper was too inept; Hawthorne too much concerned with interior states of mind. (His characters, DeForest claimed, "are as probably natives of the furthest mountains of Cathay or of the moon as of the United States of America.") The only novel possibly worthy of the distinction, he felt, was *Uncle Tom's Cabin* (1852), for at least Harriet Beecher Stowe attempted to portray a diverse range of characters who could in some sense be taken as representative of several culturally distinct regions of the United States.

The war, of course, had also brought regional differences to the fore, and Americans discovered new enjoyment in listening to native voices with accents different from their own. Western humorists like Mark Twain and Bret Harte popularized this new style for a mass audience, even as they comically exaggerated the distinctions between foolish city slickers and sharp-witted prospectors or riverboat men, whose dialects and crude manners usually convey superior vigor and force. A host of other writers also began to examine regional subcultures with meticulous care, and an expanding range of literary periodicals—*The Atlantic, Harper's Monthly, Scribner's, Lippincott's, The Galaxy, The Century*—provided lucrative new outlets for these writers. It might almost be said that the nationalizing tendencies provoked by the war simultaneously created a vogue for LOCAL COLOR WRITING, which nostalgically recreated regional peculiarities of dialect, custom, and landscape that an increasingly standardized culture was likely to efface. Writers from almost every section of the country can be identified with this movement, which reached its apex roughly from 1870 to 1900. Sarah Orne Jewett and Mary Wilkins Freeman captured the loneliness of rural New England. Joel Chandler Harris created his folk-tale hero Uncle Remus on a Georgia plantation. Kate Chopin and George W. Cable explored the Cajun bayous of Louisiana. Edgar Watson Howe and Hamlin Garland examined the pitiless, windswept life of the midwestern prairies. Even this very partial list suggests the diversity of material that American writers were taking up for the first time.

Not coincidentally, many of the principal realist writers began their careers in journalism (Twain and Howells, for example) or through the genre of travel writing (DeForest and James). Journalism and travel writing both place great value on the close observation of surface details, the deliberate accumulation of facts and evidence, all of which allow the writer to form and express comparative judgments based upon observable realities instead of preconceived ideas. Unlike earlier American writers, whose uncritical veneration for Europe often reached ridiculous extremes (such as Washington Irving's sentimental depictions of English country life in *Bracebridge Hall*), the generation of realists who came of age during the Civil War actually spent a good deal of time there; and they tended to be quite critical of European culture. Certainly Mark Twain's *Innocents Abroad* (1869) demolished the romantic view of Europe as an almost holy place. But other, more temperate assessments—such as Howells's *Venetian Life* (1866) and *Italian Journeys* (1867) or James's *Transatlantic Sketches* (1875)—also approached their subject matter with critical sensitivity.

Major Authors

Walt Whitman (1819–1892)

Although many literary historians extol Walt Whitman's Preface to the 1855 Edition of *Leaves of Grass* for establishing the high watermark of American Romanticism, his poetic practice nevertheless anticipates fundamental aspects of realistic art. Taking Emerson at his word (in "The American Scholar" [1837]), Whitman wanted deliberately to "embrace the common . . . to explore and sit at the feet of the familiar, the low." Many of his most memorable poems record the everyday prospect of a stroll down Broadway, where he can survey and catalog the hurrying swarm of ordinary human faces. Others celebrate the material stuff of everyday American life. In his "Song of the Exposition" (1876), Whitman conjures the westward course of Calliope (the classic muse of epic poetry) by tracing her steps from the foot of Mount Olympus all the way to Philadelphia, where he finds her at the Great Centennial Exhibition, "install'd amid the kitchen ware!"

Whitman's profoundly democratic inspiration sometimes led him to the brink of despair, however, as he watched the noble possibilities of the war squandered by machine politicians and corrupt officials during the first administration of Ulysses S. Grant. In *Democratic Vistas* (1870) he berated his countrymen for leaving unfulfilled the promise of freedom for which so many others had sacrificed their lives. "I say we had best look our times and lands searchingly in the face," he warned, "like a physician diagnosing some deep disease. Never was there, perhaps, more hollowness at heart than at present, and here in the United States."

■ ■ **PREFACE TO WHITMAN'S** ■ ■
LEAVES OF GRASS
In his Preface to *Leaves of Grass*, Whitman urges his readers to

> *love the earth and sun and the animals, despise riches, give alms to everyone that asks, stand up for the stupid and crazy, devote your income and labors to others, hate tyrants, argue not concerning God, have patience and indulgence toward the people, take off your hat to nothing known or unknown or to any man or number of men, go freely with powerful uneducated persons and with the young and with the mothers of families, read these leaves in the open air every season of every year of your life, re-examine all you have been told at church or school or in any book, dismiss whatever insults your own soul, and your very flesh shall be a great poem and have the richest fluency not only in its words but in the silent lines of its lips and face and between the lashes of your eyes and in every motion and joint of your body.*

Whitman's tendency to encompass the whole world in his poetry is also exemplified in this highly romantic passage.

Paradoxically, Whitman's emergence as a public poet of democracy did not always have a positive effect on his work. In 1855, Whitman had affirmed that "the proof of a poet is that his country absorbs him as affectionately as he has absorbed it." But his readers' enthusiasm for him was never fully reciprocal. Increasingly sensitive to the threat of public scandal, occasioned by charges of obscenity that were leveled against certain portions of *Leaves of Grass*, Whitman began to edit out many of the more provocative poems and to revise those that remained. At the same time, the close-knit band of Whitman's most devout followers began to remake his public image by publishing essays in praise of his work. In place of the radical visionary of the early years, we find The Good Gray Poet (the actual title of the most significant of these volumes, which appeared in 1866), the sage and prophet of democratic America. Like many other realist writers who followed, Whitman could not completely reconcile his commitment to American ideals with the role of public artist that he was obliged to accept.

William Dean Howells (1837–1920)

Though born on the Ohio frontier and deprived of a traditional education, William Dean Howells deliberately groomed himself to become an author whose graces would be recognized and esteemed by the famous intellectuals of New England. When the editors at the *Atlantic Monthly* accepted his first poem in 1860, he was overjoyed. "The truth is," he affirmed, "there is no place quite so good as Boston. . . !"

▪ ▪ ULYSSES S. GRANT ▪ ▪

While President Ulysses S. Grant was himself an honest man, his administration (1869–1877) was riddled with scandals, including:

- Crédit Mobilier. Two stockholders of the Union Pacific Railroad, Congressman Oakes Ames and Thomas Durant, formed a dummy construction company called Crédit Mobilier, which was supposed to finish the final 600 miles of the railroad. As a result of the scheme, Union Pacific stockholders and the government lost millions of dollars. Ames was able to keep the scam going by bribing several congressmen.

- Black Friday. In 1869, Jim Fisk and Jay Gould tried to corner the gold market. This means they tried to buy so much gold that they could manipulate its price. The president's brother-in-law was in on the plot and was supposed to keep Grant from finding out. Fortunately, Grant did find out and acted to remedy the situation but not before many people lost a lot of their money.

- Whiskey Ring. The government placed high taxes on alcohol in order to help pay some of the expenses of the Civil War. Treasury Department employees took bribes to issue tax stamps for much less money than they were worth.

In addition to romantic poems, young Howells also authored a campaign biography for Abraham Lincoln. In exchange, after the Republican victory in 1860, Howells was appointed as the American consul to Venice. From Europe, Howells began sending back stories about Italy, which appeared in Boston newspapers. Howells's travel sketches (collected later in *Venetian Life,* 1866, and *Italian Journeys,* 1867) brought him prestige, and he was invited to join the staff of the *Atlantic Monthly* shortly after coming back to America. In 1871 he rose to become that magazine's chief editor.

For the next ten years, Howells was in a position to redefine the contours of American literary life. By opening the pages of the *Atlantic* to a wider range of talents—including writers as unalike as Mark Twain and Henry James, two of his lifelong friends who otherwise had nothing much in common—Howells wanted to democratize the world of letters. Likewise, Howells used his editorial power to champion the virtues of literary realism, which he defined with characteristic simplicity as "nothing more and nothing less than the truthful treatment of material." Howells in his own day scandalized many readers because of his willingness to tackle subjects such as divorce (*A Modern Instance,* 1882), the corruption of business ethics (*The Rise of Silas Lapham,* 1885), social inequality (*A Hazard of New Fortunes,* 1889–90), and interracial marriage (*An Imperative Duty,* 1892).

Maintaining those artistic priorities while at the same time seeking acceptance from the literary establishment of New England put great strain on Howells's political sensibilities. Never completely abandoning the frontier values of simplicity and social equality that he had absorbed during his Ohio boyhood, in novel after novel Howells contrasts the freedom and spontaneity of characters from western or rural backgrounds with the conventionality of eastern city dwellers whose social veneer, however smooth, cannot conceal their snobbery. In fact, the author's favorite target was none other than Boston, a city, he remarked in *A Chance Acquaintance* (1873), "that would rather perish by fire and sword than be suspected of vulgarity."

In the 1880s, Howells transferred his publishing allegiances to the New York house of Harper and Brothers, with whom he established profitable connections that continued until the time of his death. For all its vitality, New York also impressed upon Howells a growing sense of social discord in American life. As the materialistic frenzy of the so-called "Gilded Age" (Mark Twain's term for the post–Civil War period) was reaching its peak, in 1888 Howells confessed to Henry James (who had long since given up on living in the United States), "I'm not in a very good humor with 'America' myself.

It seems to me the most grotesquely illogical thing under the sun; and I suppose I love it less because it wont let me love it more. I should hardly like to trust pen and ink with all the audacity of my social ideas; but after fifty years of optimistic content with 'civilization' and its ability to come out all right in the end, I now abhor it, and feel that it is coming out all wrong in the end, unless it bases itself anew on a real equality." Howells's skepticism assumed narrative form in *A Hazard of New Fortunes*, which began its serial run in *Harper's Weekly* the following year. New York exposes Howells's characters to brutal new facts—poverty, inequalities of status that make a mockery of democratic principles, the real power of capital to destroy whatever it touches. Henry James recognized that the book was "simply prodigious"; its author would never write a better one.

Henry James (1843–1916)

EPITAPHS rarely capture the essence of a man's life, but the inscription on James's tombstone in Cambridge, Massachusetts, is an exception. "Novelist / Citizen of Two Countries / Interpreter of His Generation on Both Sides of the Sea." Those fifteen words are perfectly justified by the voluminous output of America's greatest writer of fiction. James authored twenty full-length novels, more than 100 short stories, plays, volumes of literary criticism, travel, and commentary on the visual arts—there was almost no dimension of Anglo-American cultural life in the nineteenth century that escaped his discerning eye.

Still, James made his way cautiously: his first serious novel, *Roderick Hudson* (1875), appeared when the author was in his thirties. Prior to that he studiously disciplined his craft through the writing of short stories, essays, and innumerable reviews—the latter, especially, schooling him in the ways of novel writing. Overall it can be said that James found contemporary novels written in English a sorry lot, at least when compared to the more systematic work of Honoré Balzac, Gustave Flaubert, and other continental writers with whom a thoroughly cosmopolitan James was readily familiar. Unafraid of such comparison, James willingly embraced the full complexity of becoming a writer in the shadow of European accomplishment. "We are Americans born," he exclaimed to a friend in 1868, "I look upon it as a great blessing; and I think that to be an American is an excellent preparation for culture. We have exquisite qualities as a race, and it seems to me that we are ahead of the European races in the fact that more than either of them we can deal freely with forms of civilization not our own, can pick and choose and assimilate and in short (aesthetically etc.) claim our property wherever we find it." Exuberantly pragmatic, James picked and chose his artistic properties, his subject matter and experimental modes of treatment, as he shuttled between the New World and the Old, and, later (after he had taken up residence in England), between London and the cities of the Continent.

The poet T. S. Eliot once remarked that James "had a mind so fine, no Idea could violate it." By this he meant that James was exquisitely skeptical of preconceived notions or supposed truths, always willing to let the felt truth inherent in his fictional situations express itself through his characters' dialogue and behavior. Although James is frequently classified as a "realist," to label him in any categorical way does a disservice to the complexity of his work. Again and again in his critical comments about the art of fiction, we find him appealing for the artist's freedom—freedom to choose his material anywhere and to devise any form of treatment appropriate to it. Any restrictive notion as to what fictional narrative is "supposed" to accomplish (moral uplift? making the reader "feel good"?) struck him as unworthy. "There are no tendencies worth anything," he advised aspiring young writers, "but to see the actual or the imaginative, which is just as visible, and to paint it. I have only two little words for the matter remotely approaching to rule or doctrine; one is life and the other freedom." In sum, "any point of view is interesting that is a direct impression of life."

How those impressions made their way into human consciousness was a problem that James took up in almost all of his books. The disciplined revolution in technique that James accomplished was made possible through his manipulation of point of view. By letting the reader see only what his characters see, James encourages us to identify more completely and sympathetically with them (e.g., *The Portrait of a Lady,* 1881). In other instances, the limited point of view invites us to consider the shortcomings of the narrator's perspective, suggesting to us lapses of judgment occasioned by social or moral blindness (most famously, perhaps, in "Daisy Miller" [1878]). The uncertain reliability of some of his narrators (in "The Turn of the Screw," 1898, most spectacularly) often makes interpretation a challenge. But these same formal qualities have also ensured James a permanent place on the roster of novelistic greats.

Near the end of his life, James had occasion to discuss his narrative techniques as he composed a series of Prefaces for the volumes of the collected New York Edition of his novels and tales that Charles Scribner published from 1907–09. Not fully appreciated at the time, the Prefaces have since achieved a singular place in modern literary criticism, fulfilling James's ambition for them to be recognized as "a sort of comprehensive manual . . . for aspirants in our arduous profession." As a novelist, James was both of and ahead of his time. James saturated his work with detailed information about the manners, morals, and class structures of his day. At the same time, however, James's literary technique made him appealing to the modernist writers of the succeeding generation.

Mark Twain (1835–1910)

No writer from this period better exemplifies its inherent contradictions than Samuel Langhorne Clemens, better known, of course, by his pen name, Mark Twain. Often contemptuous of the false pretenses of gentility and refinement—Twain's celebrated use of VERNACULAR, or everyday, language confirms this—he also yearned for the security of a luxurious perch among the eastern establishment, as any visitor to his fabulous mansion in Hartford, Connecticut, can quickly see.

Although it is commonplace to associate Twain's initial rise to fame with the vogue for southwestern humor propelled by the exaggerated tall tales of western writers, such as Artemus Ward and Bret Harte, his greatest debt might well be to Phinneas T. Barnum, the incomparable publicist and showman of the nineteenth century. Like him, Twain knew that there was a sucker born every minute—if not more frequently. Gullibility is everywhere in Twain's work, especially along the banks of the Mississippi River, where townsfolk from Missouri, to Arkansas, to Louisiana all seem more than willing to be taken in by the enchantments of strangers from foreign places. However unscrupulous they are, the King and the Duke from *Huckleberry Finn* betray a powerful side of Twain's character, sharing his cynicism about others' need to believe in ideal sentiment and their susceptibility to the effects of inflated rhetoric. When they parody Shakespearian language in their play, "The Royal Nonesuch," they demonstrate the extent to which most Americans have accepted a false ideal of "Culture": if it sounds high-falutin', it must be superior and, therefore, worthy of respect. Civilization everywhere in Twain is a sham.

Beneath Twain's satire, however, there is a current of fatalism. However much his most admirable characters resist or defy the constraints of social convention, they seldom can escape it completely. Throughout *The Adventures of Huckleberry Finn*, for example, Huck is constantly obliged to compare himself with Tom Sawyer and to define himself in relation to what Tom insists is proper. The painful truth of this juxtaposition comes out most clearly in the novel's final section, in which, significantly, Huck actually becomes Tom (at least in name) and surrenders his own moral vision of

African American humanity to his friend's perverse romantic games. *Pudd'nhead Wilson* leaves the reader at a similar dead end, morally, as the real distinctions between slavery and freedom collapse in desperate futility. In *A Connecticut Yankee in King Arthur's Court*, all of Hank Morgan's plans for human progress culminate in what we would now call genocide. If only it were not so terribly funny!

Science, Culture, and the Emergence of Naturalism

Twain's drift toward a recognition of forces superior to human will allies him with other writers from the late nineteenth century who rejected what they perceived to be the timid middle-class boundaries of realist art. Stephen Crane, Jack London, Frank Norris, and Theodore Dreiser all could appreciate the realists' love of detailed observation, but their fiction works to undermine the delicate interplay of individual will and social circumstance that we typically find in works by James and Howells. While the realists stressed the interdependence of character and environment, their successors presume a more deterministic relationship between the two, seeing the forces of heredity and economics as exerting overwhelming pressure on human destinies.

Aspiring to the supposed objectivity of science, the proponents of NATURALISM took their cues from Darwin, portraying characters trapped by cause and effect. Whereas in James's fiction money often seems to have a potentially liberating effect on the consciousness of his characters, in Norris it becomes an impersonal force that warps and controls the individuals it touches. In *McTeague*, for example, Trina's obsession with money invites her to cram gold pieces into her mouth and jingle them about. Later she climbs into bed and lets her hoard of cool gilded coins wash over her flesh.

Similar passivity affects the characters in most naturalistic fiction. Theodore Dreiser's Carrie Meeber rocks endlessly in her favorite chair, motion that goes nowhere. Stephen Crane's Maggie drifts through the grimy streets of the Bowery, eventually drowning herself to escape poverty and sexual degradation. Jack London's characters—animal or human—are always within earshot of the Call of the Wild and, therefore, prone to become captives of instinct. The naturalist universe is indifferent to human wants and needs. Religion provides no solace because God has disappeared. As Henry Adams observed in his *Education*, in the modern world the Dynamo (the term Adams uses to refer to mechanization) had supplanted the Virgin Mary (the term Adams uses to refer to religion) at the center of human consciousness. Instead of cathedrals, we build skyscrapers, which we now know, after September 11, 2001, we also see collapse.

2. Slave Narratives and Race Relations

Slaves first came to North and South America in the 1500s. Spanish and Portuguese settlers first brought them from western Africa as part of their expanding economic and political empires. Other countries joined in the trade later. Jammed into the holds of ships, chained down, many died on the voyage, but more survived. In this way, millions of people were imported, mostly to South America, but at least half a million came to North America as well. After 300 years the practice of slavery was well established, and it is necessary to look at a few works before 1860, the start of this volume, to understand the works that followed.

The conditions of their coming were inhumane, and the treatment enslaved people received once they arrived was inhumane as well. We know the details of how they were treated only by chance. Slave owners were not interested in such documentation, and since most slaves could neither read nor write and were purposely kept from acquiring those skills, personal accounts of slave life are rare. Perhaps a dozen personal accounts called SLAVE NARRATIVES were discovered and published, some during the lives of their authors, some afterward.

In one of them, from 1789, Olaudah Equiano, brought from West Africa to Barbados, describes the unimaginable horrors of the voyage to the West Indies. "I was soon put down under the decks, and there I received such a salutation in my nostrils as I had never experienced in my life, so that, with the loathsomeness of the stench, and crying together, I became so sick and low that I was not able to eat." Equiano recounts tortures; the slightest disobedience was punished by beatings and mutilation. Slaves were whipped; ears were cut off; women were raped.

Slaves in the South tried to run away, sometimes successfully, or to carry out small acts of rebellion, such as stealing food or losing or breaking tools; some, such as Nat Turner of Virginia, rebelled more spectacularly. In 1831 Nat Turner, believing that the spirit of Christ directed him to become a martyr, led an open insurrection. Turner and his peers rampaged through Virginia, killing over 50 whites. Before being hanged, he told his story. His narrative, spoken rather than written, reveals a sense of tragic destiny and intelligence that reads today very differently than it did in 1831.

Acts such as Turner's helped bring the issue of slavery to the forefront of American consciousness, making slavery the central domestic issue of the era. Those who believed that slavery ought to be illegal were called ABOLITIONISTS; not surprisingly, most of them were northerners. As the century approached midpoint, the country was clearly heading in the direction of Civil War. In 1860 the state of South Carolina attempted to secede from the United States with the intention of forming a separate country with other slaveholding states. When the federal government, identifying itself with the non-slaveholding North, balked, the War Between the States began.

Two of the most influential books in the literature of abolitionism, the movement that led up to this war, were *The Narrative of Frederick Douglass* (1845) and *Uncle Tom's Cabin* (1852) by Harriet Beecher Stowe. The first, like Equiano's, is an example of THE LITERATURE OF WITNESS—that is to say, it is told by someone who has seen conditions firsthand. Although the book had great authority, it did not sell as widely as Stowe's novel. Both books, however different, are read with interest and sympathy today.

The Narrative of Frederick Douglass (1845)

The Narrative of Frederick Douglass is an intensely personal book, told in the voice of someone who has experienced the horrors of slavery firsthand. Douglass spends the first three chapters detailing the particulars of slave life on the Maryland farm where he was born. With natural literary instinct, Douglass explains at the start that slaves are denied a sense of their own existence, having no family names, not being told their own birth dates, separated early on from their mothers, and, in some cases, denied knowledge of their own fathers. Of possessions Douglass has practically none, slave children being given "two coarse linen shirts" a year.

If slaves are denied personal identity, the mistreatment visited upon them is intensely personal. Men are whipped. In the case of women, the torment is often allied to sex and possession. After describing his Aunt Hester as "a woman of noble form, and of graceful proportions," Douglass relates that when his master found her in the company of another man—that being her only "offense"—"he took her into the kitchen, and stripped her from neck to waist" and beat her severely. While this scene of sexual jealousy occurs, young Douglass is hiding in a closet, out of fear. The African American experience was a compound of depersonalized sex and violence.

Christianity was a dangerous force for slaveholders. Masters often kept the idea of Christianity from their slaves, for fear of suggesting an alternative existence outside the plantation. The farm of Colonel Lloyd, where Douglass passed his first years, was self-contained, and gave "the appearance of a country village." Instead of a heaven beyond that farm, slaves aspired to a substitute heaven on it, working in the "Great House Farm."

Douglass explains that slaves, denied open expression, develop a complex, private communication. What is said slave masters understand one way, slaves another. Apparently happy or meaningless songs by slaves working in the field express misery; this secondary meaning is known only to the singers.

Douglass's life changes when, at the age of seven, he is sent to the house of his master's relatives in Baltimore. *The Narrative* moves from the country to the city, where Douglass's experience is enlarged. He sees the possibility of a new kind of life. Unwittingly, he is led into knowledge. His eyes are opened.

The mistress in his new household, Mrs. Auld, is innocent; she does not understand how slaves are supposed to be treated, according to their masters. Meaning well, she begins to teach Douglass to read and to write. Her husband, worldly and corrupt, stops her. "Learning," he explains, "would *spoil* the best nigger in the world . . . it would forever unfit him to be a slave." Knowledge means power and understanding. Thus, the young Douglass can now fully understand injustices he has witnessed. The opposition of ignorance and knowledge, of slave and master, of black and white, Douglass then expresses using RHETORICAL BALANCE—that is, in a series of similarly constructed

■ ■ HOLIDAYS FOR SLAVES ■ ■
Holidays were a crucial time of year in the life of slaves. In the period between Christmas and the New Year no planting or harvesting was possible, and freedom from routine carried the danger that slaves might be tempted to consider a life of other than servitude. Accordingly, slave owners used holidays to further their own ends. Frederick Douglass in his *Narrative* describes the psychological means of enslavement that abetted the physical enslavement. This was enslavement at its subtlest and most devious: slaves were encouraged to make merry and stay drunk during the Christmas season.

"These holidays serve as conductors, or safety valves, to carry off the rebellious spirit of enslaved humanity. . ." The purpose was "to disgust the slave with freedom, by allowing him to see only the abuse of it. . . Thus, when the slave asks for virtuous freedom, the cunning slaveholder, knowing his ignorance, cheats him with a dose of vicious dissipation, artfully labeled with the name of liberty. The most of us used to drink it down, and the result was just what might be supposed: many of us were led to think that there was little to choose between liberty and slavery. We felt, and very properly too, that we had almost as well be slaves to man as to rum."

clauses. "What he [Mr. Auld] most dreaded, that I most desired. What he most loved, that I most hated. That which to him was a great evil, to be carefully shunned, was to me a great good, to be diligently sought. . . ."

It is one of the ironies of *The Narrative of the Life of Frederick Douglass* that Mr. Auld is proved correct. Knowledge *does* ruin a slave because the slave then knows that another life exists. Douglass's reader is on the side of this "ruin" and sees it as a good. There is no turning back from knowledge. Moreover, her husband's prohibition alters Mrs. Auld too. She becomes as cruel as he. Slavery not only destroys the lives of those it enslaves but also of those who do the enslaving.

As Douglass enters the world of language, he becomes an active person, capable of thinking and of taking charge of his life. When circumstances force him back to the Maryland plantation of Colonel Lloyd, the journey gives him a second glimpse of freedom. "My determination to run away was again revived. I resolved to wait only so long as the offering of a favorable opportunity. When that came, I was determined to be off."

When he returns to the plantation, he has a new master, Captain Auld—a relative of the Baltimore Auld, who finds Douglass to be rebellious and who sends him away for a year to a so-called "nigger-breaker," a Mr. Covey, a farmer of exceptional harshness who specializes in subduing stubborn slaves.

After his year with Covey, Douglass is sent out to live in comparative ease on the farm of a Mr. Freeland. (Douglass's names are obviously appropriate: an earlier overseer was named Mr. Severe.) Even though Freeland is the best master he has ever had, nothing now will suffice but liberty. After an escape plot involving forged letters fails, Douglass is returned to Baltimore, where he works as a caulker in a shipyard. Under his new conditions of employment, he is given relative freedom but is required to relinquish to his owner his entire salary. He has achieved a kind of liberty but is still in economic slavery. He has become an idealist, satisfied with nothing less than absolute freedom. "Whenever my condition was improved, instead of increasing my contentment, it only increased my desire to be free."

At this point *The Narrative of Frederick Douglass* passes from a narrative of the past into one of the present. Douglass becomes less specific, providing fewer names and places. After pretending to accept the economic servitude imposed upon him, he runs away. He refuses to divulge certain facts in his book. "How I did so,—what means I adopted,—what direction I traveled and by what

mode of conveyance,—I must leave unexplained." To detail the op-
erations of the UNDERGROUND RAILROAD, the system of safe houses
and secret routes which enabled runaway slaves to arrive in northern cities, would be to endanger the lives of the people supporting abolition. (In his third autobiography, written many years later,
Douglass does give some names and specifics.)

In the final paragraphs of *The Narrative,* Douglass reveals that
after settling in New Bedford, Massachusetts, and working as a free
man for a while at the same job at which he slaved at in Baltimore,
he has become a PROPAGANDIST for antislavery, lecturing and writing
on this topic. This is both liberation for him and a statement of the
tragic power of slavery. His life is still dominated by the overpower-
ing institution he has escaped, although he has been able to as-
sert the intellectual ability of African Americans and so establish for
himself a valid public identity.

In his lifetime Frederick Douglass was an ICON, a symbol of
freedom in general. He died in Washington, D.C., in his seventies.

Incidents in the Life of a Slave Girl (1861)

Written shortly before the Civil War, Harriet Jacobs's *Incidents in the
Life of a Slave Girl* also stresses its authenticity as literature of witness. The title page pronounces, "Northerners know nothing at all
about Slavery. They think it is perpetual bondage only. They have no
concept of the degradation involved in that word Slavery."

Calling herself Linda Brent, Harriet Jacobs focuses on the sexual
abuse of black women by their white owners. Linda tells of the un-
wanted advances made by her master, Dr. Flint. Only a COMMUNAL struc-
ture saves Linda; that is, she is helped by the community of women
around her. Her aunt, well thought of and apprised of the goings-on in
her neighborhood, prevents Dr. Flint from acting on his desires.

By desperate maneuvering and by hiding—for seven years in
a small room in the attic of her grandmother's house—Linda suc-
ceeds in evading Dr. Flint. Almost discovered in one of her rare
outings into the world, she is forced to flee north. However, Linda
is now a runaway slave. As such, under provisions of the Fugitive
Slave Act of 1850, she is subject to seizure and transportation
back to her former master. Living at that time with a Mrs. Bruce,
Linda receives word that Dr. Flint has died. Dr. Flint's son-in-law,
however, a Mr. Dodge, who has inherited the doctor's property, lo-
cates Linda in New York.

A crisis ensues. Mrs. Bruce proposes to buy Linda her freedom. The price is $300. Linda prefers that Mrs. Bruce not buy her.

"I wrote to Mrs. Bruce, thanking her, but saying that being sold from one owner to another seemed too much like slavery; that such an obligation could not easily be cancelled. . . ." For Linda, the cause is larger than the individual, even if the individual is herself. Notwithstanding, Mrs. Bruce pays the $300. Linda's feelings are mixed. She has gained the freedom she has desired but at the price of capitulating to the general evil.

Such complexities reflect the impossibility of partial solutions to the problem of slavery. Pride and defiance, even for Jacobs, is colored by guilt. Of her alliance with Mr. Sands she writes, "I know I did wrong. . . . Still, in looking back, calmly, on the events of my life, I feel that the slave woman ought not to be judged by the same standard as others." Yet in the midst of these complexities, Harriet Jacobs's book stands as an instance of feminine solidarity. The love that she bears for her children is matched by the "love, duty, [and] gratitude" she feels for Mrs. Bruce. The uneasiness that pervades *Incidents in the Life of a Slave Girl* is, paradoxically, one of the features that keeps it fresh and gives it its narrative vitality.

Walt Whitman and Other Civil War Literature

With Walt Whitman, one of the most original and affecting poets America has produced, we move away from the realistic approaches toward slavery toward the TRANSCENDENT. Whitman was not much interested in the particulars of slavery; he was interested in the grand sweep of America—its history, the variety of its population, its democratic ideals, the way that America, considered as a whole, was itself a collective grand vision in which everyone had a part.

African Americans appear in Whitman's poetry, as, indeed, almost everything about life in America made its way into his embrace. The "Drum Taps" section of *Leaves of Grass,* Whitman's collected poetic work, describes his most intimate link to the Civil War. Here, Whitman describes "the squads gather[ing] everywhere by common consent and arm" and the gathering of all the United States in its preparations for war and later the effects of the war on the soldiers:

> The neck of the cavalry-man with the bullet through and through examine,
> Hard the breathing rattles, quite glazed already the eye, yet life struggles hard,
> (Come sweet death! be persuaded O beautiful death!
> In mercy come quickly.)

Frederick Douglass
The author and crusader faces the camera, in about 1860, with a
mixture of shrewdness, stubbornness, and indomitable will. For this
photo Douglass has dressed in the typical middle-class clothing
of the nineteenth-century. Photographs were formal affairs in that
period and could require the sitter to hold one position for three
minutes or more.

■ ■ ■ ■ THE FUGITIVE SLAVE ACT OF 1850 ■ ■ ■ ■

One of the most contradictory aspects of slavery was the issue of fugitive slaves. What was the status of a slave who escaped from a slaveholding state into a nonslaveholding one? Laws were passed in 1793 and 1850 to regulate this dilemma, although as early as 1643 the New England Confederation tried to deal with the question. In response to the 1793 law, Indiana (1824), Connecticut (1828), New York (1840), Vermont (1840), Pennsylvania (1847), and Rhode Island (1848) passed laws either guaranteeing a fugitive the right to a trial by jury or granting freedom. At this point the South demanded more effective federal legislation. In 1850, in exchange for other measures, the Fugitive Slave Act was passed. As a result of this legislation, fugitives could not testify in their own behalf; there would be no jury trials; penalties were imposed on people who aided slaves in escaping and marshals were set up to enforce the laws and could themselves be punished if they refused to do so; and the identity of the slave and the facts of the escape could be attested to by others on behalf of the people involved. A commissioner who found that a slave was in effect a fugitive was paid $10; a commissioner was paid $5 when he judged that the fugitive was free.

The Fugitive Slave Act, in effect, enforced slavery throughout the United States. The law was very unpopular and actually increased the number of abolitionists. Moreover, northern states began to pass Personal Liberty Laws to negate the effects of the Fugitive Slave Act. These Personal Liberty Laws were a prime reason cited by South Carolina in its decision to try to secede from the Union, an act that began the Civil War.

In addition, the Civil War produced memorable battle literature, such as General Sherman's and Grant's *Memoirs,* and the diaries of Mary Chesnutt. In terms of immediate contemporary impact, however, nothing mattered as much as one single novel of 1852.

Uncle Tom's Cabin (1852)

Uncle Tom's Cabin was a phenomenon in publishing history. Not since Tom Paine's *Common Sense* was a book so influential. Worldwide, Harriet Beecher Stowe's novel sold more copies in its day than any other book except the Bible.

It came at a crucial moment in American history. The sectional crisis between slaveholding and nonslaveholding states was at its height; southerners declared that they would never accept

Five Generations of a Slave Family
Outside their rough wooden cabin, this African-American family poses for a portrait. It appears that their clothing is their Sunday best, donned for the occasion of the picture. Farming implements are at hand, though discreetly in the background. For obvious economic reasons, owners of slaves encouraged large families.

domination by the nonslaveholding North. In exchange for an agreement to permit new territories to determine their position on slavery, the North had been forced into agreeing to the Fugitive Slave Act of 1850, which set penalties for not returning runaway slaves. The slaves had no say; they were denied jury trials, a decision that the Supreme Court would reinforce in 1857 with the *Dred Scott* decision, which refused blacks the right of citizenship.

All these events reinforced the timeliness of *Uncle Tom's Cabin,* so that in 1862, when Harriet Beecher Stowe met Abraham Lincoln, the president said to her, "So you're the little woman who started this great war."

Unlike the slave narratives, *Uncle Tom's Cabin* is the product of an outsider. Harriet Beecher Stowe was the daughter of a famous New England clergyman, Lyman Beecher, and although on occasion Stowe writes a scene in which there are only black characters, in most of the action where black characters figure, a white person is also present. Stowe's ability to connect to the reading audience in the nineteenth century, almost exclusively white, accounts in part for the book's astonishing sales. Its power as a DIDACTIC work is also responsible for its popularity.

Uncle Tom's Cabin uses the Bible to reinforce its presentation of the wrongs of slavery. Each chapter contains an overt or buried bibical reference. If religion only gradually becomes a conscious reference point in *The Narrative of Frederick Douglass* or *Incidents in the Life of a Slave Girl,* it is an integral part of the prose of *Uncle Tom's Cabin.*

Uncle Tom's Cabin is sometimes seen as simplistic because it makes complex issues seem easier to understand than they are. However, the characters in the book are faced with difficult, defining choices that the novel presents in all their complexity.

Although some readers claim that *Uncle Tom's Cabin* glorifies SUBSERVIENCE, not all characters in the narrative accept their lots as slaves. After she hears of Shelby's impending sale, for example, one orphan slave, Eliza, flees with her child. She crosses the Ohio River into freedom. Stowe writes that the river "lay, like Jordan, between her and the Canaan of liberty on the other side." The comparison is to the flight of the Israelites into the land of milk and honey as described in Exodus. Freedom is paradise.

Eliza is pursued by the slave hunter Tom Loker. He is wounded and falls into the hands of kind Quakers, whose society the novel idealizes. Although many troubles await Eliza, by the end she is reunited with her faithful husband in Canada, away from the strife-torn United States, and eventually settles in Africa.

▪ ▪ ▪ ▪ THE CONFEDERATE CONSTITUTION AND THE SLAVE ▪ ▪ ▪ ▪
The Confederate States set up a Constitution modeled on the United States Constitution of 1787 with the difference that slavery was permitted. The word "negro" appears three times in the document, showing how the confederacy wanted to control the institution of slavery.

The importation of negroes of the African race from any foreign country other than the slaveholding States or Territories of the United States of America, is hereby forbidden; and Congress is required to pass such laws as shall effectually prevent the same. (Article I, Section 9)

No bill of attainder, ex post facto law, or law denying or impairing the right of property in negro slaves shall be passed. (Article I, Section 9)

The Confederate States may acquire new territory; and Congress shall have power to legislate and provide governments for the inhabitants of all territory belonging to the Confederate States, lying without the limits of the several Sates; and may permit them, at such times, and in such manner as it may by law provide, to form States to be admitted into the Confederacy. In all such territory the institution of negro slavery, as it now exists in the Confederate States, shall be recognized and protected by Congress and by the Territorial government; and the inhabitants of the several Confederate States and Territories shall have the right to take to such Territory any slaves lawfully held by them in any of the States or Territories of the Confederate States. (Article IV, Section 3)

Uncle Tom—one of the book's two enduring symbols—is the devoted, religious slave who will not steal away. "Mas'r always found me on the spot—he always will. I never have broken trust, nor used my pass no ways contrary to my word, and I never will." Faced with the comparable kindness of Mr. Freeman, Frederick Douglass flees. Tom, on the other hand, embarks upon an odyssey toward martyrdom. It begins at the hands of the slave trader Haley. Tom is to be sold "down the river," meaning he will be sent to a plantation further south on the Mississippi where masters treat slaves more cruelly.

In a scene as convenient and melodramatic as any in nineteenth-century fiction, Tom saves the life of a rich child thrown overboard on a steamboat. The consequence is that the child's father, Augustine St. Clare, purchases Tom from Haley. St. Clare intends to make

Tom a coachman. Little Eva, the child Tom saved, is a devout Christian, and she and Tom develop a close bond in a household that Stowe presents as an EXPOSÉ of the kindly southern family. The ideal life at St. Clare's is only a temporary reprieve.

Tom is sold to Simon Legree, who, like Tom, leapt from the pages to become an icon. Tom's humility and refusal to whip another slave (recalling a similar moment from *The Narrative of Frederick Douglass)* infuriate Legree. "I'm willin' to work night and day, and work while there's life and breath in me; but this yer thing I can't feel it right to do;—and, Mas'r, I *never* shall do it,—*never!"*

These are the harshest episodes in the novel. Tom's Christianity sends Legree into impotent fury. He becomes a sadist with a whip. For such behavior on the part of slave owners, unfortunately, historical evidence exists.

As Legree becomes more deranged, Tom begins to have visions of a redemptive sort. Legree whips Tom to death. "Ye poor miserable critter!" Tom tells Legree, in a scene where he re-enacts Jesus on the cross. This is the suffering that, in the nineteenth-century sentimentalism, ennobles. "There ain't no more ye can do! I forgive ye, with all my soul!"

Uncle Tom's Cabin is no longer the force in American life and letters that it was. It presents some solutions to the problem of race relations that later centuries reject. It is hard to argue that Stowe envisions equality for the races if Eliza and her family cannot remain in the United States. Moreover, such a resolution avoids the problem it was intended to address and glorifies an ethnic purity impossible to achieve—and undesirable in any case. And Tom himself is now a symbol for a subservient slave, a traitor to the cause of true liberation.

Abraham Lincoln (1809–1865)

The man most associated with the addressing the problem of slavery in the nineteenth century was Abraham Lincoln. It is, therefore, somewhat surprising to learn (as one of the quotes below illustrates) that Lincoln came to the position that slavery was wrong only after trying other positions. He did, however, sign the Emancipation Proclamation (1863), an act that freed all the slaves in rebellious states and put conditions in place to hold the union together as one free country, with laws designed to protect every citizen.

His manner was remarkably plain spoken in an age of flamboyant oratory. Henry Clay, Daniel Webster, and Stephen Douglas were known for rhetorical flourishes and sometimes for their grandiloquent style. Lincoln, by contrast, presented himself as a common man. Doubtless he was posturing somewhat, but of the plainness of his diction there can be no doubt: The writing is there.

His biography—a characteristically American one ("from log cabin to White House")—almost overshadows the distinction of his prose. Not an intellectual as such, Lincoln read the Bible, *Hamlet,* and *Macbeth* obsessively. From his inner resources and these literary antecedents, Lincoln built a distinctive prose style characterized by the simultaneous use of two rhetorical devices: PARALLELISM and BALANCE. (One thinks of Douglass!)

This sentence from a letter Lincoln wrote to the newspaper editor Horace Greeley, illustrates both qualities: "If I could save the union, without freeing any slave, I would do it; and if I could save it by freeing all the slaves, I would do it; and if I could save it by freeing some and leaving others alone, I would also do that." The repeated conditional clauses that start with "if" gather force by highlighting the slight variations within them, while the similarity of the main clauses— "I would do it"—binds the sentence together.

> ▪ ▪ LINCOLN AND DOUGLASS ▪ ▪
> Eventually Frederick Douglass established himself as a prominent thinker and crusader for the rights of African Americans. However, he was still excluded from important events. It was customary, after a president was inaugurated, for the White House to be opened for a reception. Douglass, who had been invited to a reception after Abraham Lincoln's second inauguration, was not allowed to enter the building. He was stopped by a policeman at the front door. However, the president asked that he be let in and shook his hand cordially. "Douglass, I saw you in the crowd today listening to my inaugural address. There is no man's opinion that I value more than yours; what do you think of it?" Douglass told him: "Mr. Lincoln, it was a sacred effort." The president smiled. "I am glad you liked it."

At the end of his most famous speech, "The Gettysburg Address," Lincoln describes the government as "of the people, by the people, for the people," three perfectly balanced, parallel prepositional phrases. At the conclusion of his second inaugural address, Lincoln writes "with malice toward none, with charity for all." Other examples abound.

The formal quality of this prose, its understated simplicity, and the loftiness of Lincoln's thought are leavened by dry wit, the frontier humor of Artemus Ward (a writer who was one of the president's favorites), and the practical attitudes that realists brought to the sentimental novel. "The Lord prefers common-looking people. That is why he makes so many of them."

■ ■ ■ ■ SLAVE AUCTIONS ■ ■ ■ ■

Following are two descriptions of slave auctions. First is an eyewitness account from Solomon Northrup, a free African American sold into slavery in 1841 after being kidnapped:

> *Next day many customers called to examine Freeman's [the owner of the slave pen] 'new lot.' He would make us hold up our heads, walk briskly back and forth, while customers would feel of our hands and arms and bodies, turn us about, ask us what we could do, make us open our mouths and show our teeth, precisely as a jockey examines a horse which he is about to barter for or purchase. Sometimes a man or woman was taken to the small house in the yard, stripped, and inspected more minutely. Scars upon a slave's back were considered evidence of a rebellious or unruly spirit, and hurt his sale.*

The second description comes from Stowe's *Uncle Tom's Cabin*. As the daughter of a minister, Stowe was especially appalled at the sexual degradation of women and the hypocrisy of believers who supported slavery.

> *Stretched out in various attitudes over the floor [the reader] may see numberless sleeping forms of every shade and complexion, from the purest ebony to white, and of all years, from childhood to old age, lying now asleep. . . . A respectably-dressed mulatto woman between forty and fifty, with soft eyes and gentle and pleasing physiognomy . . . has on her head a high-raised turban, made of a gay red Madras handkerchief, of the first quality; her dress is neatly fitted, and of good quality, showing that she has been provided for with a careful hand. By her side, and nestling closely to her, is a young girl of fifteen,—her daughter. She is a quadroon, as may be seen from her fairer complexion, though her likeness to her mother is quite discernible. . . . These two are to be sold tomorrow, in the same lot with the St. Clare servants; and the gentleman to whom they belong, and to whom money for their sale is to be transmitted, is a member of a Christian church in New York, who will receive the money, and go thereafter to the sacrament of his Lord and theirs, and think no more of it.*

The tensions that resulted in the Civil War were the dominant problem of mid-nineteenth-century America; the perfect prose for dealing with them was Lincoln's. It seems the natural outcropping of American common sense and straightforwardness.

3. Mark Twain (1835–1910)

Mark Twain was the most revered author in America in his day, and his reputation lives on today after his death. His remarks—for example, "the report of my death was an exaggeration"—are still quoted, his work continues to appeal to a spectrum of readers—common people, historians, and scholars, and his image is still a familiar one.

Clemens did not start out to be a writer. His experiences with printing led to a job with the *Territorial Enterprise* in Virginia City, Nevada, where he began mixing reportage with humorous articles and sketches of the rough-and-ready Southwest. He signed himself with a term borrowed from his riverboating says; "Mark Twain" means two fathoms of water, safe for boating.

From the beginning and to the end Twain's writing depends on doubleness; there are two sides to his nature: He was attracted to what he mocked. A deep impulse led Clemens to adopt the PSEUDONYM, "Twain."

Associating with the humorist Artemus Ward and adapting Ward's comical dialogue and exaggeration—staples of frontier humor—Twain wrote his first masterpiece in 1865, "The Celebrated Jumping Frog of Calaveras County."

Twain and Regionalism

Based on a folk tale that had been circulating for a dozen years, "The Jumping Frog of Calaveras County" is a BURLESQUE. A stranger arriving in town looking for one person instead encounters another: Simon Wheeler, who tells him about the antics of a man named Smiley and his jumping frog. Wheeler's is obviously a TALL TALE. No one can force five pounds of buckshot into a frog and keep it alive as Smiley is said to do.

"The Jumping Frog" is a letter to Artemus Ward both to acknowledge a debt and to show that Twain can beat Ward at his own game. The story gains by twinning its voices. One voice belongs to the formally proper narrator ("I inquired after your friend Leonidas W. Smiley, as you requested me to do . . .") The second belongs to the talkative, ungrammatical narrator, Simon Wheeler ("Thish-yer Smiley had a mare—the boys called her the fifteen minute nag, but that was only in fun, you know, because, of course, she was faster than that . . ."). These two animate the tale by playing off each other. The story throughout uses the comical, regionalist spellings of Ward, who was fond of writing "grabd," "vilently," and "umbreller" to mimic local accents.

Twain works in wider significances. Smiley's frog is named Dan'l Webster, after the American orator and secretary of state (1782–1852). The colloquial contracting of "Daniel" and the absurdity of naming a frog after a distinguished man take the self-important Webster down a peg. Behind the exuberant humor is satire. The power elites of the East are nothing more than frogs full of buckshot.

Calaveras County provides the regional contrast. These folksy characters, Twain implies, are the real America—shrewd, conniving, down-home folks, with a laughable touch of absurdity. The town where the action occurs is called "Boomerang." At home in the mud and swamps, Jim Smiley is an instance of local color, a town character.

The form of Twain's brief sketch is another double: paradoxically and comically open and closed. Although it begins as a formal letter to Ward, Wheeler's voice takes over, unspooling itself as though it could go on forever—life, at least for these characters, has no clear aim. This notion is reinforced by the blind ends Twain introduces: The narrator is not seeking the "Smiley" he happens upon; the one he wants has the ridiculously mixed name (and title) of Rev. Leonidas W. Smiley. The story stops—not ends—when the narrator cuts the flow off, for Wheeler is ready with another story of Smiley and his "yaller one-eyed cow that didn't have no tail only just a short stump like a bannanner."

Other writers of humor wrote under pseudonyms, though ones less deeply revealing than Twain's: Ward, Petroleum V. Nasby, Orpheus C. Kerr ("office seeker"), Josh Billings, and Bill Nye. Their stock-in-trade consisted of mangled syntax, funny, realistic

■ ■ **MARK TWAIN AS PRINTER** ■ ■

Mark Twain is one of many famous American writers who did not obtain a college degree. (Melville, Hemingway, and Faulkner are others.) His early education consisted of the reading typical in nineteenth-century schools—moralistic stories in *McGuffey's Readers*, for instance, where a prudent boy finds many uses for a bit of packing thread his improvident companions discard.

Twain's real education came at his early job. "I became a printer and began to add one link after another which was to lead me into the literary profession," he wrote. "One isn't a printer ten years without setting up acres of good and bad literature, and learning—unconsciously at first, consciously later—to discriminate between the two."

These early experiences account for the prevalence of printers in Twain's fiction. In *Huckleberry Finn*, the Duke and the King steal into a print shop and easily make handbills for the Royal Nonesuch; comically bad typography abounds in *A Connecticut Yankee in King Arthur's Court*, and the hero of the last work Twain worked on, *No. 44, The Mysterious Stranger*, is a printer's apprentice.

dialogue, tall tales, folk legends, extraordinary characters, local scenery, and the characteristic device of the YOKEL who deflates the self-important and pretentious. Where other writers might employ one or two of these elements, "The Jumping Frog of Calaveras County" has them all, with an exhilarating sweetness in the barb.

Early Travel Books and *The Gilded Age* (1873)

After the modest success in volume form of *The Jumping Frog of Calaveras County* (1867), Twain journeyed through Europe and the Middle East, writing newspaper dispatches about countries he visited. These he compiled into *The Innocents Abroad* (1869). His method of composition assured that the result would be a jumble of a book composed of discrete incidents, but readers in 1869 were less interested in form than in Twain's humor. After writing this book, he composed a similar one based on his experiences out west as a young man, *Roughing It* (1872), one of the last looks at America before the age of big business that began after the Civil War.

None of Twain's succeeding books except his next would be set in contemporary times; they return to a simpler time, less dominated by corporate greed and organized corruption. Written with Charles Dudley Warner, *The Gilded Age* (1873) is a satire of power and greed that gave its title to an era. It is the first Washington novel, and its indictment of Washington power politics is not dated: Back deals; power games; corrupt, hypocritical congressmen and hangers-on; opportunists; power-struck social climbers; fools; and criminals are as prevalent now as they were then.

The Adventures of Tom Sawyer (1876)

Called by its author a "hymn to boyhood," *The Adventures of Tom Sawyer* consciously isolates itself from the adult world and goes back to 1835. It focuses on a mildly mischievous boy, nine years old, raised by his husbandless aunt in a village on the banks of the Mississippi River.

The story is constructed around three semirelated episodes in the midst of which Tom "plays, runs, and hides": the murder by Injun Joe of Dr. Robinson; Tom and his companions' holiday on Jackson Island; and the hunting of Injun Joe with the recovery of a lost treasure. Tom's existence is defined by the pranks he plays on the adult world. Superficially, they appear to be acts of rebellion but actually they reinforce his identity with the adults rather than separate him from them.

The most famous episode makes this point. Tom turns his punishment of whitewashing into an occasion for commerce. He starts the day as a bad boy, playing hooky, and ends it as a capitalist. The goods he gains parody material culture, the jimcracks of the Gilded Age. Within Tom's world they are wealth itself: "a half-eaten apple, a kite, a rat . . ." (followed by a list of thirteen more items).

If, throughout this book, Tom consciously becomes the hero of his own adventures, it is tempting to call Huckleberry Finn the antihero, but in this book he is part of Tom's fantasy. He has a life that Tom Sawyer thinks he envies: "Huckleberry came and went, at his own free will. He slept on doorsteps in fine weather and in empty hogsheads in wet; he did not have to go to school or church, or call any being master, or obey anybody . . . he could swear wonderfully." Huck and Tom are Twain's most interesting twins, doubles who interact with each other richly.

The real outsider in *The Adventures of Tom Sawyer* is Injun Joe. His alienation is the result of prejudice. The robbing and killing Tom Sawyer feigns Injun Joe ennacts. The separation from accepted society that Tom believes he envies is forced on Injun Joe. After he has committed the crimes for which he is pursued, he disguises himself as a deaf and dumb Spaniard, further acting out the rejection.

The book cannot condone Injun Joe's evil acts, but in Injun Joe's background is serious injustice. Without pursuing the implications of these details and becoming a realistic book in the manner of *Pudd'nhead Wilson, The Adventures of Tom Sawyer* cannot face up to Injun Joe nor to the serious topic of race relations that hovers around its edges.

The Adventures of Huckleberry Finn (1885)

Many of Twain's other books, especially *The Adventures of Tom Sawyer,* connect to *The Adventures of Huckleberry Finn,* but the book can be read on its own and has been in more languages than any other American title, including *Uncle Tom's Cabin.* The first sentence is magical—"You don't know about me without you have read a book by the name of 'The Adventures of Tom Sawyer,' but that ain't no matter." Slangy, ungrammatical, friendly, pliant, expressive, Huck's language is wholly new. A host of books afterward have adopted not Huck's Missouri dialect but the idea of youthful VERNACULAR. *The Catcher in the Rye* by J. D. Salinger (1951) and *The Adventures of Augie March* by Saul Bellow (1953) are two. Twain was there first.

Mark Twain and Society
Twain celebrating his 70th birthday in 1905 in New York, at the then-fashionable Delmonico's restaurant. Although by this time on the lecture circuit to clear his debts, Twain continued to travel among the elite and fashionable. Notice the elegant dress and ladies' hairstyles of the day, the ornate wall covering, velvety drapes, and glowing gaslight, adding to an atmosphere of elegance.

Form and Plot

As Huck tells his story the book reveals itself to be a PICARESQUE novel. In fifteenth-century Spanish literature the hero of such a tale was called a picaro and he was usually a villain or rogue. Huckleberry Finn, as an outcast and one who identifies with villains ("I might get to be a murderer myself one day"), is a modern picaro.

The picaresque form requires incidents that follow chronologically—there are few flashbacks in *The Adventures of Huckleberry Finn.* This looseness suits Twain, his long travel books being casual assemblages. In fact, Twain previews the style in his introduction, stating, "Persons wishing to find a plot . . . in it will be shot."

Of shooting and violence there is plenty. Huck leaves Miss Watson and the Widow Douglas, where he was situated at the end of *The Adventures of Tom Sawyer,* when he hears that his alcoholic father has returned to claim him. Sensing that his father is after his money, he sells his property to Judge Thatcher. For a while Huck lives with his father in the woods. When his father starts to beat him, he fakes his own death and runs away to Jackson's Island, where he meets Jim, a slave who has also run away. They intend to go North, where Jim will be free, but they are split up in a fog and pass the crucial junction. Huck is taken in by the Grangerfords, who are feuding with the Shepherdsons.

After a battle in which some on either side are killed, Huck escapes, rediscovers Jim, and the two head off but are joined by two con men, the "King" and "Duke" who practice a variety of shady schemes to obtain money. As the plot becomes unraveled, Huck and Jim escape only to discover that the King and Duke have sold Jim.

In the moral climax of the book, Huck decides to rescue Jim, even though he believes that doing so means putting his soul in danger. After seeing the King and Duke tarred and feathered, Huck finds Jim on the farm of Silas Phelps. Arriving there, Huck discovers that Sally Phelps is Tom Sawyer's aunt. Huck pretends to be Tom. Tom arrives and takes the identity of his brother Sid. Under Tom Sawyer's direction, the boys carry out an elaborate scheme to free Jim, in the course of which Tom is shot. Tom reveals that Miss Watson has died and freed Jim in her will. Jim reveals that the dead man in the floating house was Huck's father. Although Huck recovers his fortune, he wants no part of being "sivilized" again, so he decides to "light out for the territory ahead of the rest."

Language

The use of language in *Huckleberry Finn* is an American first. Other literature had used first-person narration, but the diction was correct speech. *The Adventures of Huckleberry Finn* revels in the less-than-proper. It finds its home outside of literary or sanctioned language, siding with common speech. Twain does not affirm vulgarity, however, or rebellion, but democracy, the democracy of the common person with common sense who stands apart from empty propriety and rote correctness.

This stance invigorates. Huck's speech is freshly responsive, with new metaphors that comprise a poetry of the common people, characterized by honesty and a lack of cant. Unromantic, realistic, Huck thinks with disarming directness, "Why can't Miss Watson fat up?" His colloquial "fat up" has a comical, startling directness. At another point Huck wakes up and writes, "It *smelt* late. You know what I mean—I don't know the words to put it in." Huck is not using "smell" in the traditional, approved way, but who has not felt what he means? His more expressive language rejuvenates.

Readers in the twentieth century have found Huck's use of one term offensive. Huck calls Jim, and other black people, "niggers." Today, 120 years after the book was published, as in 1885 when the first American edition appeared, "nigger" is an offensive word. However, Huck does not use it to denigrate or "put down" Jim. Historically, that was the term used in 1840, when the action of the book occurs.

Moreover, Huck knows that Jim is his most constant and loving companion, whom he himself loves, in a world where love is rare. To contrast Huck's feelings, the reader can look at the truly prejudiced man in *Huckleberry Finn:* Pap Finn. Twain loads the initial description of Huck's father with one word, repeated six times: "There warn't no color in his face, where his face showed; it was white, not like another man's white, but a white to make a body sick, a white to make a body's flesh crawl—a tree-toad white, a fish-belly white." Pap Finn hates the "mulatter" who can vote and who is a "p'fesser in a college," who is "most as white as a white man" and who wears "the whitest shirt . . . you ever see." Pap Finn's mispronunciation of "mulatto" and "professor" are signs of an ignorance that the reader does not forgive, as the reader is not bothered, say, by Huck's not knowing how to spell the common name "Jackson" or for getting the facts of English history mixed up. Pap Finn tries to insist on a superiority that is unjustified and cruel and that points to his lack of sympathy for others, but Huck Finn's heart is pure.

Themes and Patterns in *The Adventures of Huckleberry Finn*

As many readers have noticed, the story is built on a central opposition: river versus land. Huck and Jim on the river are free; they live easily in a world of potential. The episodes on land are another

▪ ▪ Poetry of The Adventures of Huckleberry Finn ▪ ▪
Twain's language in this book has an exquisite, fresh beauty, as in Huck's
description of morning on the Mississippi River.

*Not a sound anywheres—perfectly still—just like the whole world was asleep,
only sometimes the bullfrogs a-cluttering, maybe. The first thing to see,
looking away over the water, was a kind of dull line—that was the woods on
t'other side; you couldn't make nothing else out; then a pale place in the sky;
then more paleness spreading around; then the river softened up away off, and
warn't black any more, but gray; you could see little dark spots drifting ever
so far away—trading scows, and such things; and long black streaks—rafts;
sometimes you could hear a sweep screaking; or jumbled up voices, it was so
still, and the sounds come so far; and by and by you could see a streak on the
water which you know by the look of the streak that there's a snag there in the
swift current which breaks on it and makes that streak look that way; and you
see the mist curl up off of the water; and the east reddens up, and the river, you
make out a log-cabin in the edge of the woods, away on the bank on t'other
side of the river, being a woodyard, likely, and piled by them cheats so you can
throw a dog through it anywheres; then the nice breeze springs up, and comes
fanning you from over there, so cool and fresh and sweet to smell on account of
the woods and the flowers; but sometimes not that way, because they've left dead
fish laying around, gars and such, and they do get pretty rank; and next you've
got the full day, and everything smiling in the sun, and the song-birds just
going it!*

matter. They represent what America has done with its freedom.
Some of the narrowness of this life is presented in the episodes
with Miss Watson and with Huck's father—the alcoholism, the sentimental repentance that fails, and the violence.

The great central parts of *Huckleberry Finn* begin with the arrival of
another set of Twain twins: the Duke and the King, two con men whose
names are never revealed. If the Grangerfords have some claims to
aristocracy, these two characters, who claim aristocratic titles, have
none at all. They are obvious frauds whom Huckleberry Finn sees
through immediately. They stay on the raft and sponge off Huck and
Jim while devising illegitimate schemes to gain a few quick dollars.

This section of the book exposes, in a broadly comic way,
the cultural and emotional limits of American society—a further
indictment of the use of freedom. The citizens of Arkansas are not

Huck Finn and Jim
Huck and Jim maneuver the raft while the Duke and the King, as befits their royal status, lie in the tent. Note Huck's primitive rudder and the unbuilt-up shoreline.

interested in the Duke and King's comically garbled imitations of Shakespeare. They want indecency ("LADIES AND CHILDREN NOT ADMITTED. . . 'If that line don't fetch them, I don't know Arkansaw.'"), and then the chance to lambaste the actors who take advantage of them as they deserved.

It is when the Duke and King see a chance to bilk a family out of its inheritance that middle-class American social life comes in for a drubbing. The Duke and the King, though transparent fakes, manage to rob the decent Wilkses by pretending to be long-awaited inheritors of a will. Unlike the Grangerfords, the Wilkses are gullible. The schlocky indulgence of Emmeline Grangerford's verse is acted out in the parochialism and emotional naiveté of the Wilks family. The King and the Duke, seeing a chance to pose as inheritors, attempt to defraud the family out of everything they own, selling property and slaves, all illegally. The mixture of crass reality taking advantage of the inherent sentimentality of the Wilkses, of trickery and "tears and flapdoodle," makes this section of the book the liveliest, rawest, and most appalling.

Huck Finn cannot stand it. "It was enough to make a body ashamed of the human race." He devises a plan to foil the King and Duke, earning the trust of the essentially warmhearted Mary Jane Wilks. As he is doing so, other inheritors arrive, probably (but not conclusively) the real ones. In the confusion, the plans unravel and Huck escapes again, hoping to be free of a civilization that works by opportunists cheating fools for the sake of a few dollars, without respect for human dignity. That is American civilization—the bitter theme at the heart of *The Adventures of Huckleberry Finn*.

Huck's Growing Emotional Maturity with Respect to Jim

The relationship between Huck and Jim, the central one in the book, acts as a contrast to that theme. There are three main stages. In the first few chapters, when Huck is still under the sway of Tom Sawyer, Jim is presented as a stereotypical black, sly and prey to superstitious beliefs, comical in the mode of some of the characters in *Uncle Tom's Cabin*. When he finds a nickel Tom Sawyer has left for him he attributes its appearance to witches. Jim tricks Huck into giving him a counterfeit quarter so his magical hairball can read Huck's future.

Jim grows in status as the story progresses. Huck consults Jim when he hears that his drunken father has come looking for him. Huck, having run away from his father and the Widow Douglas, finds that Jim has also run away. The two meet on Jackson's Island. The implication is clear: Jim, a man valued only for the labor that can be got from him, becomes the father of Huckleberry Finn, a boy whom society finds of no account.

The second stage in Huck's relationship to Jim occurs in Chapter XV. Huck has been fooling Jim into thinking that Jim dreamed something that actually has occurred. Jim comes to understand that he has been tricked. In a short, upbraiding speech of simple dignity, Jim concludes, "Trash is what people is dat puts dirt on de head er dey fren's en makes 'em ashamed." To his credit, Huck sees the human outrage he has committed. "It was fifteen minutes before I could work myself up to go and humble myself to a nigger—but I done it and warn't never sorry for it afterwards, neither." This moment signals a conscious shift. They have become equals for that moment.

The Duke and King force the final stage in Huck's connection to Jim in Chapter XXXI. The two "rapscallions" betray Huck and Jim by selling Jim to a farmer named Silas Phelps. This utterly antihumane action is part of Twain's criticism of nineteenth-century capitalism. The Duke and King do something brutally cruel but entirely within the law, for Jim is property.

When he finds out what has occurred and has located Jim, Huck debates with himself. Should he inform Miss Watson where Jim is so that he will be sent back to her? He knows that Miss Watson will "sell Jim down the river." The reader knows that informing is a morally reprehensible action because slavery is wrong, but according to the laws of the time and to Huck's conscience, it is the right thing to do. Huck opts for what he thinks is wickedness. In effect, he gives his life for Jim: "All right, then, I'll go to hell."

This is the moral climax of the book. It is presented with the same irony that informed Huck's judgment of Emmeline Grangerford's poetry.

Readers may not always agree with Huckleberry Finn's judgments, but they are on his side—until the last third. The disappointment many readers feel in the ending of *The Adventures of Huckleberry Finn,* when Tom and Huck devise the plot to rescue Jim, comes from what they see as Huck's selling out to Tom Sawyer. After being willing to "go to hell" for Jim, Huck then agrees to play with him, needlessly delaying his release—all made worse by Tom Sawyer's revelation that Jim has been free all the while. To make Jim suffer through such childishness is for Huck, the realist, to accede to Tom Sawyer, the romantic. It could be done only by someone unaware of another person as a human being.

Explanations have been offered to justify this final part of *The Adventures of Huckleberry Finn,* none wholly convincing. Perhaps one can say that just as Huck feels pity for the Duke and King when he sees them tarred and feathered by irate townspeople whom they have probably bilked, so he does not wholly reject Tom. He does make a cool appraisal of his friend in the final paragraph: "Tom's . . . got his bullet around his neck on a watch guard for a watch, and is always seeing what time it is." Tom is stuck in himself, in time, in the gaudy trappings of civilization.

There is no place for Huck. "Aunt Sally she's going to adopt me and sivilize me and I can't stand it. I been there before." This is the end to Huck's story, always a misfit in a society in which it is hardly worthwhile to fit. However final Huck's rejection of "sivilization," he refuses with such engaging humor that the bitterness goes down almost without the reader's noticing. Jim is now free, although it is beyond the book, and perhaps beyond Mark Twain, to imagine a civilization that could accommodate him and "the only friend he has now."

Admired in its time and judged by its author as his best, *The Adventures of Huckleberry Finn* was not the book most readers preferred in the late nineteenth and early twentieth century, but today it ranks with the poems of Whitman and Dickinson, Hawthorne's *The Scarlet Letter*, Melville's *Moby-Dick*, Fitzgerald's *The Great Gatsby,* and Faulkner's *The Sound and the Fury* as one of the texts that define America.

Pudd'nhead Wilson (1894) and Later Works

After at least one more notable book, *A Connecticut Yankee in King Arthur's Court* (1889), came Twain's final, tragic statement on human relations. *Pudd'nhead Wilson* (1894) is set in 1835 in Dawson's Landing, a town like the St. Petersburg of *The Adventures of Tom Sawyer.* There are three main characters: David Wilson, mockingly dubbed Pudd'nhead, the outsider, the protoscientist who collects fingerprints of everyone in Dawson's Landing out of interest in this then-new science; Roxy, the almost-white slave who gives birth to a boy whom she calls Chambers (after "valet de chambre," or room servant); and Chambers himself, called Tom throughout most of the narrative, who is switched for the son of Roxy's master, Percy Dricscoll. The true heir disappears for most of the narrative.

The novel depicts the corrosive effects of environment, especially that of the southern gentleman. Here Twain's dislike for

the proud aristocrat who was slavery's most ardent supporter is
at its most virulent. Roxy's son is spoiled by the proud, "cavalier-
like" father who raises him. Tom (in reality a person of mixed race)
believes that being white and rich he has the right to whatever he
wants. He attends Yale. He develops the vices of a rich man; he
runs up gambling debts. Shocked when his mother reveals to him
that he is black, he murders his step-father to cover his debts,
contriving to place the blame on Italian noblemen visiting Dawson's
Landing. Wilson, however, solves the murder with fingerprint evidence. The roles of the deposed heir and slave child are righted in
a solution tragic for everyone. The slave, the Yale graduate, is sold
down the river; the rightful heir, raised as a slave, cannot adjust to
his proper position.

Half the length of *Huckleberry Finn,* the novel has the force
of a PARABLE. It demonstrates that it is too late to repair the damage done by slavery. Even if circumstances would permit blacks
and whites to change place, human failings and the environment
spoil good intentions. Truth, usually the property of outsiders
like Pudd'nhead mocked for their sagacity, cannot salvage this
situation.

Although Mark Twain wrote one masterful short story, "The
Man That Corrupted Hadleyburg" in the final fifteen years of his
life, the writing closest to him he deemed too shocking and pes-
simistic to publish. The main instance is a manuscript unfinished
at his death, *No. 44, The Mysterious Stranger.* Here the hero has a
number instead of a name. He works as a printer's apprentice but
has magical, devilish powers. The loose narrative, set in Austria in
1490, is a brutal anti-Christian questioning of the purpose of existence. It ranges throughout all history, viewing human foibles and
greed from an exasperated, godlike perspective. "Oh, this human
life, this earthly life, this weary life! It is so groveling, and so mean;
its ambitions are so paltry, its prides so trivial, its vanities so child-
ish; and the glories that it values and applauds—lord, how empty!"

Twain was certainly correct that publishing *No. 44, The Mysterious Stranger* would have altered his reputation as a humorist
by revealing his profound despair. If here and in other books, he
disdained the artificial smoothness that leads to aesthetic triumph,
Mark Twain achieved something arguably more important: the authenticity without which writing is at best a trivial exercise.

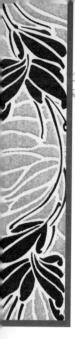

4. Urban Writers and Internationalism: Alger, Howells, James, Wharton

Emerging from the Civil War in 1865, America found itself more diverse, apparently more unified and certainly more powerful than before. Cities attracted growing numbers of people seeking economic and cultural opportunities. America became less insular and more aware of itself as a nation internally and in the world. Its literature reflected these changes, in both simple and sophisticated ways.

Horatio Alger (1832–1899)

Horatio Alger was one of the writers who helped fix America's sense of its opportunities. By the nineteenth century an ARCHETYPICAL American experience had been determined; certain qualities of the "American dream" had been established. The idea was that America was a land of opportunity. Honesty and striving resulted in success. These notions were embedded deeply in the American character, from Benjamin Franklin's *Autobiography* (written in the 1780s) onward. Franklin tells how as a young man he arrived in Philadelphia penniless but ambitious and how, by living temperately, he managed to become a successful printer and publisher, thereby representing the embodiment of an American ideal.

Alger, an ex-minister, wrote popular fiction for boys. His novels are FORMULAIC; they follow a pattern, as do detective stories, gothic novels, romances, and TV sitcoms. The formula that Alger followed, in almost 100 books, from the 1860s (*Ragged Dick,* 1868) to the late 1890s (*Jed the Poorhouse Boy,* 1899) was Franklin's, the story of rags to riches.

Ragged Dick of New York, an orphan, sleeps in a cardboard box ("The Box Hotel," he calls it), shines shoes, returns change honestly, earnestly studies to better himself, and proves courageous and trustworthy in trying circumstances, saving the drowning child of a rich man. Scores of other Alger heroes do similar things. Success and a worthy girl result. This is DIDACTIC fiction, meant to teach its readers a lesson and to inspire them to be better people.

Alger's novels were consumed by the millions. They had an effect far beyond their literary impact. They also established a pattern against which mature, realistic fiction, especially fiction concerned with business or commerce, set itself.

Philadelphia, 1897
A crowded cobblestone street bustles with trolley cars and horse-drawn carriages, as was typical in urban environments at the turn of the century. Hatted men—wearing bowlers, skimmers, and caps—watch the busy scene.

■ ■ ■ ■ HORATIO ALGER SEEN TODAY ■ ■ ■ ■

One writer against whom some realists pitted themselves was Horatio Alger. Alger made an appealing target for several reasons. Even given his juvenile audience, Alger's style was simplistic and especially wooden. His characters were one dimensional—all good or all bad. The plots in his novels depended upon coincidences and patently planted situations, as when the virtuous Ragged Dick saves a rich man's daughter from drowning in the Hudson River. The morality of his stories was so simple-minded that anyone with a slight experience of life could see its falsity. Poor boys are not always honest and rewarded nor are rich boys almost invariably spoiled and greedy.

Finally, Alger was a tempting figure because, notwithstanding all his deficiencies, his books were consumed by the millions. They represented the values that people believed when they were first starting to read and that they would continue to believe only to their detriment.

Of course, most readers of Alger's novels did not mistake them for journalism or for accounts of the "real world." However, the values Alger's books affirmed—thrift, honesty, persistence, fidelity—were and are unquestionably good ones; the more serious issues of how and if to hold to those ideals is a suitable one for writers of realistic fiction. It is certain that Alger's virtues are likely to be only shallowly planted if the fiction that idealizes them is not tested against an experience of the complex life in which they must be practiced.

Alger lives on. In 2010 there is a Horatio Alger Society, which gives out an annual Strive and Succeed Award.

William Dean Howells (1837–1920)

Like his friend Mark Twain, Howells was from the Midwest, but he gravitated to the East, to GENTEEL literary surroundings. After holding the editorship of America's most prestigious literary magazine, *The Atlantic Monthly,* Howells concentrated on his own fiction. In 1882, he published the first of the novels on which his reputation as a writer and American REALIST, someone who tries to imitate the complexities of real life in fiction, depends, *A Modern Instance.*

The character study of a shallow, ambitious Boston journalist, Bartley Hubbard, *A Modern Instance* details the circumstances that lead Hubbard to betray his decent, loving wife Marcia, to squander his energies, and finally, after Marcia divorces him, to flee to Arizona. The realistic element, new to fiction when the novel was published, was the candid treatment of marriage and divorce.

Howells's next major work of fiction proved his most lasting. In *The Rise of Silas Lapham,* published in 1885, the same year as *The Adventures of Huckleberry Finn,* Howells produced the first serious novel about an American businessman. It shows the role commerce played in modern American life.

The Rise of Silas Lapham (1885)

The Rise of Silas Lapham divides into three parts, with the most telling scene occurring in the center. Silas Lapham, from Vermont, has made a fortune in the mineral paint business. Vigorous, ingenuous, unsubtle, ungrammatical ("it don't"), Lapham sees nothing tasteless or defiling about painting advertisements on any convenient rock. His qualities are put forth sympathetically in the first chapter of the novel, where he is interviewed by Bartley Hubbard of *A Modern Instance.*

In the first third of the story, Lapham is a successful businessman. Crude, proud, and forceful, he faces what seems an agreeable dilemma. Now that he has made money, how should he live? What is the American dream for? It is first of all a social problem. With his realist's eye for detail, Howells lists the stages of wealth.

The plot links the Lapham and Corey families. Bromfield Corey's son Tom applies to Lapham for a job. At this point, the novel with its carefully balanced sympathies, seems to favor the vigorous, sustaining efforts of American business by suggesting that without the fuel from commercial enterprise a fully satisfying, dynamic life of self-fulfillment is impossible.

Bromfield Corey seems to admit as much. The reader cannot help being on the side of young Tom Corey opting for engagement, refusing to spend his time "wasting money," and carefully husbanding his resources to avoid sordid commerce. Then another complication arises: Corey has fallen in love with one of Lapham's daughters.

In the second third of *The Rise of Silas Lapham* these family and commercial alliances draw the two social groups closer. Howells shows, with comic flair, how different the Laphams and the Coreys are.

In the crucial chapter, upon which Howells lavishes his talents as a writer of A COMEDY OF MANNERS, a work that explores the different habits and customs of different social classes, the Coreys throw a dinner party for the Laphams. Without realizing that they are doing so, the Laphams commit every social mistake possible.

■ ■ ■ ■ REALISM AS A LITERARY GENRE ■ ■ ■ ■

John Updike, the twentieth-century critic and novelist, wrote of Howells, "As a practitioner and critic, he sought to hold himself and other writers to a standard of realism that rose above the romantic exaggerations and implausible adventures that characterized popular fiction in his day and, indeed, in ours." Updike is pointing out that, even today, much American fiction depends upon fairy-tale endings, where poor girls marry rich young men and live happily in worlds where good and evil are easy to sort out and choose among. Realism, however, looks at the conditions under which wealth is obtained and the ways in which money impinges on character. The hard choices that wealth forces on those who possess it and the way in which money changes its possessors are themes of *The Rise of Silas Lapham* and realistic fiction in general. It is significant that in fairy tales, and in the works of Horatio Alger, the story is over once the characters are rich. "Money changes everything," runs a popular song. Realism shows how.

However, realism is not only social. It is psychological as well. Henry James dramatizes the ambiguity of human motivation. People do not always know or say what they mean, even if they want to. In James's late novella, *The Spoils of Poynton,* young impoverished Fleda Vetch "colours" and tells Mrs. Gereth that she will not marry her handsome, philistine son Owen "because he's too stupid!" The reason for her blushing and the strength of her exclamation is that she thinks she loves Owen and would gladly marry him were circumstances right. Later, given the chance, she holds back, supposedly because she is unsure that Owen has broken with his fiancée, even though Owen has not spoken to Mona for weeks. Does Fleda really love Owen?

Lapham is not wholly lost, however, and manages to take something from the evening. He appreciates some keen observations on the subject of love by the minister, the Rev. Sewell, although he finds himself unable to express himself in kind. Sewell's point, that passion is presented in frivolous novels as though it is the end point to a relationship whereas in life it is only the start, also sounds like Howells', and Lapham's approval of it identifies the author with his creation.

Lapham's social failure is the turning point. Howells lets only one chapter pass before Tom declares his love for Penelope, distressing both families. The Coreys must accept a woman they dislike, of a class beneath them. And Penelope's sister has,

Newspaper Boys in Boston

This is Boston, but it could be any city. These are the enterprising youths that Horatio Alger (1832–1899) liked to depict. As in *Luke Walton: Or, The Chicago Newsboy*, published in 1889, this was the sort who would sell papers that men of finance (in Dreiser's *The Financier*) would learn the news that would affect world markets. In the age before radio, newspapers were the chief means by which citizens were informed of the doings of the greater world.

to this point, believed Tom was in love with her. It is natural that a
novel occupied with ethical and social concerns moves toward the
church. At this point *The Rise of Silas Lapham,* which has been a
comedy about business and social manners, becomes a moral tale.

The moral tone drives the final third of *The Rise of Silas Lapham.*
Chapters XX to XXVII depict Silas Lapham's failure in business, the
loss of his house, and his moral ennoblement.

Attracted as he was to the new America and its bustling cities, by 1890 Howells had said what he had to say. It was not in
him to espouse radical social thought or the naturalistic ideas of
the writers such as Stephen Crane and Frank Norris whose careers
he generously promoted. He was a "man of letters." Every serious
writer of the last half of the nineteenth century knew Howells, and
Howells knew everyone. His tastes were wide-ranging and CATHOLIC;
he was the only writer equally at home with Mark Twain and Henry
James, two polarities of nineteenth-century American sensibility.

Henry James (1843–1916)

Even more than Mark Twain, Henry James is a study in himself.
Possessed of one of the subtlest minds ever to write fiction,
James, over the course of his 40–year career as a writer, developed in breadth and sophistication of technique. He was born
into a distinguished family: His brother William was the American
pragmatist philosopher. Although he maintained connections to
America, Henry James was increasingly drawn to Europe and the
year before his death became a British subject.

As with Twain, the label "realist" applies to James but is too
small to accommodate all his qualities. Insofar as he is a realist,
he espouses PSYCHOLOGICAL REALISM, an attempt to show realistically
how people think and feel. The physical world—furniture, houses,
paintings, lawns, teacups, landmarks—is meticulously described
as the case requires, but James's primary interest is not in surface
things but in the way his characters understand that surface. The
most significant moments in his books occur when his characters
see past the privileged settings that most of them inhabit.

For all James's love of Europe, James's fiction often values
what may be loosely called American traits of character: forthright-
ness, honesty, openness, and a belief in individual freedom. It
frequently makes those affirmations by putting Americans in a
European setting. What the city was to Alger and Howells, Europe
and world civilization were to James. His view is larger and more
sophisticated, but it is fundamentally of the United States.

Just as James himself was a displaced American, many of his characters live abroad. The hero of his early novel *The American,* with the pointed name of Christopher Newman, becomes involved, in Paris, in courting a half-French, half-English widow. The family of the widow does not like Newman, but they tolerate him because he is rich. The theme of the novel is that Americans can bridge the cultural difference between their own country and Europe only partially and with difficulty. Newman's refusal to act on what he knows testifies to his fineness of sensibility—and, in general, holding back in James's fiction often means more than acting. These are not simple Alger characters. They are complex beings actuated by conflicting, many-faceted values, and they cannot immediately see the right thing to do.

Perhaps the landmark novel of James's early period is *The Portrait of a Lady* (1881). It too is the story of an American abroad, an impoverished INGÉNUE named Isabel Archer. This attractive, high-spirited, proud, intelligent woman refuses to marry a titled Englishman because she values her independence and wants to realize herself more fully. For the same reasons she also rejects an American suitor, Caspar Goodwood. An invalid Englishman, also in love with her, but too ill to marry, makes her financially independent. On a trip to Italy she meets an American widower, a DILETTANTE, Gilbert Osmond. Isabel, accustomed to living among people of taste and probity, cannot see Osmond's shallowness or his gold-digging. After they marry, she sees him clearly and moreover discovers that Osmond's child was not by his wife. She is approached one last time by Goodwood, one of the open, honest Americans who contrast, sometimes favorably, sometimes not, to the indirect, ironic Europeans. Goodwood urges her to leave her husband, but she turns him down a second time out of duty to her stepdaughter and pride, returning to her unhappy marriage.

James's writing career was not based on producing popular books, as was Mark Twain's, but upon developing fictional technique, most especially the LIMITED OMNISCIENT POINT OF VIEW, in which a story is told from the third person but restricts itself to what that person can see or know. This perspective gives James great flexibility. It provides him with focus and concentration while enabling him to make the larger comments of which his characters may be unaware; he may let a reader feel how intensely drawn Lambert Strether in *The Ambassadors* is to a young woman, for example, and at the same time let the reader see how that woman's and Strether's limitations mesh.

The Turn of the Screw (1898)

James's concern for the perspective from which stories are told can be seen in one of his most widely read, *The Turn of the Screw.* Almost all critical discussion of this story focuses on the narrator.

Like many ghost stories, *The Turn of the Screw* is a story-within-a-story, with an introductory chapter establishing that we are about to read a manuscript "in old faded ink." Such distancing is useful. Extraordinary events become more plausible when the evidence is presented indirectly, enabling the writer simultaneously to tell the tale and to claim that it is only that which someone else has said.

The frame also establishes a point of view, namely, that of a nameless governess, writing some years after having been put in charge of two beautiful children, Miles and Flora, on an isolated estate in England. Having been hired by an attractive bachelor, the governess is told "that she should never trouble him never, never." All difficulties and problems she must meet herself as best she can. At first all seems well. Then the governess begins to suspect that the children are being haunted by ghosts, a suspicion that eventually leads to the death of one of the children.

For 30 years after it appeared, *The Turn of the Screw* was read in one way, as a terrifying story in which ghosts work their will against small charges whom the governess tries in vain to save. The story understood this way has two tragedies: the governess's and that of Flora and Miles. The governess's best efforts are defeated by the greater supernatural forces bedeviling the children. This little corner of the world, as in many ghost stories, is ruled by forces whose evil endures. Moreover, unlike other stories, in which good triumphs over evil, in this one evil triumphs over good, adding to the potency of the tale.

However, a few years after James's death, Professor Harold C. Goddard of Swarthmore College proposed that the governess was insane. Goddard noted that James never showed that anyone other than the governess sees the ghosts. All the evidence for their existence comes from her. In other words, the reality of *The Turn of the Screw* resides in the mind of the governess. "But perhaps the most interesting and convincing point in this whole connection," writes Goddard, "is the fact that the appearance of the ghosts is timed to correspond not at all with some appropriate or receptive moment in the children's experience but very nicely with some mental crisis in the governess'."

This idea, propounded by the American critic Edmund Wilson and by others, has been amplified in succeeding years by scholars who have seen as a motivation for the governess's delusion her repressed sexual attraction to her employer, displaced onto Miles. Other fiction that James was writing around the same time, such as *What Maisie Knew* (1897), suggests answers to this question, but they are not conclusive. A final answer is impossible.

That there are two equally coherent, mutually exclusive, persuasive interpretations has ensured that the story will endure. The ambiguity that characterizes the work of Henry James returns the reader to the problem of how a reader or living person understands experience. We are given the evidence. However, what is the reality of that evidence? How do we process it?

James remains the most sensitive delineator of the differences in culture between America and Europe. He is still America's most international writer. In his books one will not find a taste for the wild and uncultivated, nor does James have the romantic's attraction toward nature; his books are urban and urbane. There are several American novels that are the equal of James's masterpieces, but overall Henry James remains the greatest master of fiction America has produced.

Edith Wharton (1862–1937): *The House of Mirth, Ethan Frome*

The writer who is closest in sensibility to James but whose work is less insistently international is his friend and sometime follower Edith Wharton. Born into a wealthy family, she focused on the social aristocracy of New York, although one of her most renowned works is set in rural New England. Less multifaceted than James, she is more of a social SATIRIST. Her incisive sense of social MILIEUX gives her work the deeply etched sharpness of realism.

Her reputation was established with her fourth book, *The House of Mirth* (1905), still one of her best known. Lily Bart is a socially ambitious woman with all the requisites for entering high society in New York: beautiful, smart, and socially adept. However, her family has lost its money, and Lily, living with her moderately well-off aunt, has no ability to imagine a life for herself beyond the luxurious one to which she has grown accustomed. Consequently, she is in search of a wealthy husband.

The opening pages of Part I of *The House of Mirth* present this dilemma by contrasting the man Lily truly loves, Lawrence Selden, a lawyer who is insufficiently rich, with the man on whom she first sets her sights, the monumentally dull, transparently manipulat-able, staggeringly moneyed Percy Gryce. At a fancy house party, Lily gambles, as is expected of guests, but she cannot bring herself to pursue Gryce, who finds someone from his own set.

In Part II a temporary reprieve comes. Lily's friend Bertha invites her to go on a Mediterranean cruise with her family. Bertha is using Lily's presence to divert her husband while she has an affair behind his back. When she chooses to end the affair, she cuts Lily off. Lily returns to New York. There she finds that her aunt has died and left her only a small sum of money.

As a result, Lily is forced to work as a hat maker. For a while she tries associating with a level of society just below the wealthi-est one, but it is not in her to compromise.

The characters in this novel are a new species of rich Ameri-cans. They are not like those who have money in *The Rise of Silas Lapham,* either crude but ethical businessmen or exhausted aris-tocrats. They are bold, vigorous, and far wealthier. *The House of Mirth* drips with gold. Lavish dinners succeed equally lavish dinners. It is a world of riches, second houses in Newport, grand proper-ties in upstate New York, Fifth Avenue townhouses, and yachts. This money is the product of the Gilded Age, when vast fortunes were made by the Rockefellers, Goulds, Morgans, and Carnegies, cutthroat industrialists who controlled markets in oil, steel, and transportation, the riches to which the pathetic young men in Mark Twain's *The Gilded Age* aspired. The Trenors have a house on Long Island, the Dorsets take cruises to Europe to show off their wealth and to spend it on the luxuries and culture that Europe could offer, rather than on American goods.

The distance between the privileged and poorer classes has become astronomical. Although there are working people in *The House of Mirth,* for the most part, they represent what people strug-gle to avoid.

New York is not the locale for one of Wharton's most famous works, the NOVELLA *Ethan Frome.* This story, which Wharton started writing in French in order to exercise her skills in that language, is set in rural Starkfield, Massachusetts. Wharton made up this name to suggest the bare, "stark" country lives of its inhabitants. They are New England Yankees, stoic, laconic, reclusive—that is, they contain their emotions, do not say much, and keep to themselves.

Like *The Turn of the Screw, Ethan Frome* frames its account as a narrative-within-a-narrative. This time the outsider who tells the story is an engineer on business in Starkfield. This man encounters

Ethan Frome, a farmer eking out a bare living from stubborn Massachusetts soil. From people in the village the engineer cobbles together the story of Ethan Frome's life. Frome has married Zenobia, called "Zeena," a shrewish, whining woman who is preoccupied with her many ailments.

When Zenobia's cousin Mattie Silver comes to live with the two, Ethan finds himself drawn to her. She is young and vibrant, a splash of color in drab Starkfield. Zenobia is quick to sense this attraction. She sends Mattie away. As Ethan is driving Mattie to the railroad station from which she is to depart, they openly declare their love for each other.

As a final farewell, they borrow a child's sled for an exhilarating ride downhill, but the joy of the ride heightens their despair. Realizing the hopelessness of their situation, Mattie proposes a suicide pact. "Ethan, I want you to take me down again . . . right into the big elm . . . so 't we'd never have to leave each other any more." As they fly down the hill in the sled toward the tree, in complete union ("her blood seemed to be in his veins"), Frome thinks of his wife, swerves, and instead of dying maims them. They are condemned to live out a long life in their bare farmhouse under the constant vigil of Zenobia.

This is a love triangle. The fateful tragedy gains from Wharton's economy. Purity, elegance of description—was ever a New England winter so cold and snowy?—realistic detail, and the sense of inevitability combine with perfection of form. The potent alliance of sex and death in the climax make it a consummate piece of fiction,

■ ■ **EDITH WHARTON'S LIFE** ■ ■

Edith Wharton was born Edith Newbold Jones in New York City in 1862. Her wealthy and cultivated family did not especially value intellectual pursuits. Women were expected to adorn the large and elegant parties that members of her social set gave. That was Wharton's early life; she married and set about showing off her husband's money. All the while she was writing, and in 1905 with *The House of Mirth* she achieved her first great success. Six years later she separated from her husband and moved to France.

From 1905 her books reveal the ruthlessness of power and social climbing. Unlike the heroine of her novel *The Custom of the Country* (1913), Wharton never had to climb the social ladder, but she saw the corrosive effects of doing so on those who felt themselves so obliged. During World War I, she organized relief aid for orphans and refugees and wrote about her visits to the front line. She was decorated by the French government.

An intimate of Henry James, she wrote more than 80 short stories and more than a score of novels. Her portrait of the leisure class and the psychological realism of her characters earned her the respect of the leading writers of her day.

■   ■   ■   ■   THE HOUSE OF A VANDERBILT   ■   ■   ■   ■   ■

Two rich New York families who were often at odds with each other were the Astors and the Vanderbilts. To gain acceptance into the society of the Astors, who had gained their fortune in Colonial times, the more recently rich Vanderbilts—William and his wife Alva—built a mansion at 660 Fifth Avenue in New York. One writer describes how the Vanderbilts spent money on a house that would let them reach the pinnacle of the social level that they desired:

It took two years for imported Italian stonecutters to frame the granite foundation, to carve the intricate panels that bordered the windows and balustrades of the third and fourth stories. Ornate decor of unicorns, sea serpents, griffins, and cupids were added to the blue slate roof with copper cresting. The entrance pavilion held an obvious message: 'fleurs de lys', along with acorns and oak leaves (fashioned into a coat of arms for the Vanderbilt family), which represented 'great oaks from tiny acorns'. Throughout the interior, one delighted in tapestries and superb French furniture (some of which had belonged to Marie Antoinette). Alva's collection of paintings included Rembrandt's 'The Noble Slav', Greuze's 'Broken Eggs', and portraits by Thomas Gainsborough and Joshua Reynolds. Perhaps the most notorious room was the two-story dining hall, where guests dined in the glow of immense stained glass windows, and felt dwarfed by the magnificent double fireplace with its elaborate carved niches that held life-sized statues and valuable porcelain vases. The intent of the room was obvious: guests were not so important; works of art would outlast them.

if not a wholly characteristic story for Edith Wharton, whose sensibility remained grounded in late nineteenth century America. Unlike James's fiction, in which those in love renounce their wishes and thereby become more human, in Wharton's universe characters are denied compensation or reward.

5. Regionalism

The writers in the previous chapter, Howells, Wharton, and especially James, were internationalists. Their fiction occurs both in the United States and abroad. One can write fiction from many perches, however; and in America a special group of writers called LOCAL COLORISTS or REGIONALISTS kept to their own immediate surroundings. Their work has the charm of a distinct place even while presenting the experiences that happen to all people, no matter where they live. All local color stories, even when the authors are writing about events contemporaneous with the times, manifest a desire to preserve a time and place that the writer feels may be threatened by the rapid changes taking place. The mood is implicitly NOSTALGIC.

After the Civil War, with its cataclysmic shift in national identity and consciousness, the United States was no longer the simpler pre-war America. This nostalgia—that life was better in a previous period—became part of the American consciousness. As far back as the writing of James Fenimore Cooper (1789–1851), with his PAEANS, to a presettlement New York state, nostalgia was part of the American consciousness; the Civil War brought that consciousness to the fore and reinforced it. It is not surprising then that local colorists flourished after 1865, when the War Between the States was over.

New England

The New England states—Maine, New Hampshire, Vermont, Connecticut, Rhode Island, and Massachusetts—have their own associated character. This fact has already been mentioned in the discussion of Wharton's *Ethan Frome;* New Englanders have to deal with harsh weather, stony ground, and a lack of natural resources, but out of these privations has come thrift, ingenuity, resourcefulness, and a restrained, withheld temperament with its own humor. New Englanders do not suffer fools gladly. They value independence. Boston, the first great American city, and Massachusetts have long been associated with culture and intelligence, Massachusetts as the site of the first Puritan settlements, and the state of the American transcendentalists.

After the Civil War, the economic and cultural center of America began to move to New York, a displacement reflected in the fiction of Melville and Howells. New Englanders, however, had their defenders. Two writers who especially associated themselves with New England were Mary E. Wilkins Freeman (1852–1930) of Massachusetts and Sarah Orne Jewett (1849–1909), who spent most of her life in South Berwick, Maine. Of these two, Jewett in particular left a significant body of work. Originally inspired by sketches of Maine written by Harriet Beecher Stowe, she wrote one memorable novel, *A Country Doctor* (1884), and one masterpiece, *The Country of the Pointed Firs* (1896).

Although sometimes called a novel, *The Country of the Pointed Firs* is a collection of interrelated stories all centering on the East Maine maritime village of Dunnet ("Done it") Landing, told by an outsider who spends her summers rooming with one of the locals. These sorts of collections of stories have become an American specialty; *Winesburg, Ohio* (1919) by Sherwood Anderson, and *In Our Time* (1925) by Ernest Hemingway are similar collections.

Through Mrs. Almira Todd, the narrator comes to know many of the local characters. One is an old sea captain. Speaking in a characteristically flat New England accent ("I wa'n't caught astern o' the lighter by any fault of mine"), Captain Littlepage in a chapter called "The Waiting Place" recounts an adventure told him by a Captain Gaffett. Marooned off the coast of Greenland, Gaffett "struck a coast that wasn't laid down or charted" and that was "two degrees farther north than ships had ever been." There he comes upon grey, foglike figures that can never quite be approached and a town that seems to be both real and illusory, "a waiting place between this world an' the next."

It is a typical sea story of a New England village, with a touch of the fantastic. The cozy atmosphere of Dunnet Landing, where everyone knows everyone else and the town seems one big family, contrasts to the illusory, far-off settlement that Gaffett has discovered. What is that town? Limbo? Purgatory? The story may recall Ulysses's voyage beyond the accepted limits of the world in Canto XXVI of Dante's *Inferno*. It is made more plausible by the apt characterization of the sea captain who recounts it and the New England sense of limitation, both illustrated by Littlepage's judgment that "'Twa'n't a right-feeling part of the world."

Weddings and funerals are the main events of most lives. From her corner of New England, Sarah Orne Jewett set forth both. She is valued today for her novels with particularly modern themes: the feminist implications of *A Country Doctor,* and her story "A White Heron" with its environmental sympathies.

The South

Of all the regions in America, that with the most complex psychological makeup is probably the South. Unlike the North, with its smaller farms and its manufacturing—eventually a concentration of factories, the South was the domain of landed gentry. Its aristocracy

■ ■ ■ ■ SARAH ORNE JEWETT'S ARTISTRY ■ ■ ■ ■
From the Opening of Jewett's Story "A White Heron"

The companions followed the shady wood-road, the cow taking slow steps and the child very fast ones. The cow stopped long at the brook to drink, as if the pasture were not half a swamp, and Sylvia stood still and waited, letting her bare feet cool themselves in the shoal water, while the great twilight moths struck softly against her. She waded on through the brook as the cow moved away, and listened to the thrushes with a heart that beat fast with pleasure. There was a stirring in the great boughs overhead. They were full of little birds and beasts that seemed to be wide awake, and going about their world, or else saying good-night to each other in sleepy twitters. . . .

This story is typical of Jewett. Sylvia, who has returned from the town back to her native land, feels an immediate identification with it. Jewett dramatizes this identification quietly: Jewett values sympathy over intellect, as Sylvia comes to protect the secrets of the heron's nest rather than expose them to the ornithologist who wants to study it.

consisted of large landholders who lived in rural gentility. It was a slaveholding region. When the South lost the Civil War, a contradictory set of attitudes came into play: shame over losing the war and to some extent over having subjugated a people because of their race, and pride: a dream of the days of lost dominance and glory. The days of elegance and sweetness were gone. No dream endures as well as one that must remain a dream. Sometimes these attitudes forced southerners into a defensive posture.

Of all the regions in the United States, the South was most affected by the Civil War. Its institutions were the most changed, and its way of life was altered in the smallest particulars. Nostalgia was more powerful than in other regions of the United States. The persistence of the past is a constant theme in southern literature. As William Faulkner famously declared: "The past isn't even the past."

Faulkner's predecessors felt similarly. Two of the most notable are George Washington Cable and Kate Chopin, both from Louisiana.

George Washington Cable (1844–1925)
Although late in his life Cable wrote shallow COSTUME DRAMAS (*The Cavalier* is an example*),* his early work, particularly the seven

stories in *Old Creole Days* (1879) and his novels *The Grandissimes* (1880) and *Madame Delphine* (1885), explore serious issues, often about the mixing of races or the extent of racial blood necessary to define a person as black or white—that is, the "COLOR LINE." The title *Old Creole Days* points to this theme without defining it precisely, a Creole being a person of mixed French or Spanish and white blood. (Later "Creole" also came to mean a person of both black and white descent.)

Kate Chopin (1851–1904)

Although a successful writer in her day, Kate Chopin gained her fame mostly in the twentieth century after her death thanks to her influential novel *The Awakening* (1899). A dramatic account of a woman's awakening to herself in all senses—individual, social, and sexual—*The Awakening* is less infused with local color than the stories for which Chopin was known in her lifetime, principally those collected in *Bayou Folk* (1894) and *A Night in Acadie* (1897). Her Catholic, complexly cultured people of Natchitoches parish speak in a multilingual, playful manner that attests to the richness of their lives.

> ■ ■ GEORGE WASHINGTON CABLE ■ ■
> AND MARK TWAIN
> Though both [writer Lafcadio] Hearn and Mark Twain had more poetry, more of the "temperament" of the artist than Cable, George Cable had a stronger intellect and more integration of character than either. He was five feet six inches tall and a good deal shorter than Clemens, and they would come on the platform together because it made the audience laugh. There is a photograph of them posing together, and it is curious to see the towering Twain, coat thrown open and hand in his pocket, gazing out at the responsive public on whose repose his self-confidence so much depends, but in moral stature not overtopping the concentrated and tiny Cable, with his trimmed beards and his mandarin mustaches, buttoned up in his frock coat, so good-naturedly sure of himself.
>
> —Edmund Wilson, *Patriotic Gore*

Chopin's personal history has come to play a part in interpreting her work. Born in Missouri, she married a New Orleans banker and lived most of her life in that city. Her father-in-law owned a cotton plantation on the Red River, scene of the Simon Legree passages in *Uncle Tom's Cabin.* Writing in a busy household and active socially, Chopin composed some of her tales in one day.

Many are brief, pointed anecdotes of less than 3,000 words. In "Désirée's Baby," Désirée's husband Armand discovers that his baby exhibits Negro characteristics. He concludes that his wife, an orphan, and, therefore, his child are of mixed racial background.

He cruelly sends his wife away. She takes the baby and walks into the swamp, presumably to die. In the last lines of the story, however, Armand, burning the effects of his past, discovers that he is of mixed blood, not his wife.

The strongest thematic element, one typical of the South, is the ever-present notion of the past haunting and dominating the present. Both Désirée's indeterminate origins, of which her mother is aware, and Aubigny's origins, affect their present lives. What Désirée thinks is the true past, leads her possibly to commit suicide (the story does not definitely state that Désirée dies). That same misunderstood idea leads Aubigny to burn the effects of his marriage. The fury and completeness of this destruction by fire—a purifying element—points to the strength of Aubigny's feelings; he wishes to disassociate himself from any taint of black blood.

Charles Chesnutt (1858–1932)

The African American novelist, short story writer, and essayist Charles Chesnutt, born in Ohio but relocated to North Carolina, superficially seems to write stories with some of the same characteristics as Joel Chandler Harris's Uncle Remus folk tales. However, Chesnutt's sociological intent is stronger. His novels, *The House Behind the Cedars* (1900) and *The Marrow of Tradition* (1901), explore the tensions between black and white. Rena Walden, the main figure in the earlier novel, must discover exactly who she is—including her race. In the latter novel, violence erupts in a North Carolina town when its complacent segregation is challenged as a result of the conflict of two families, one white, one black, who are related.

Chesnutt began his writing career as a financial reporter and later became an accountant while continuing to write short stories. His first major publication, and still one of his most renowned tales, was the first story by an African American to appear in the *Atlantic Monthly,* "The Goophered [bewitched] Grapevine." Told by a white man, a Yankee, who seeks to buy a vineyard in North Carolina that will produce "the luscious scuppernong" grape, the story quickly shifts to the main narrator, Uncle Julius McAdoo, an African American living on the premises.

The story is a kind of local color; it is a parable of the position of African Americans after the war who are forced to live on the land by their wits. Their history and folklore are richly comic. They know within limits how to manipulate whites, their former "oberseahs."

Only now coming back into the high reputation he enjoyed during the early part of the twentieth century, Chesnutt was not only a novelist and a short story writer, but a powerful expository writer as well. One of his best known essays, "What Is a White Man?" (1889), directly addresses the issue of the color line in research that quickly makes a shambles of the subject and reduces it to absurdity. What defines a white person, Chesnutt asks; what makes a white person white? What defines a black person? How much black blood can a white person have and still be considered white? In 3,000 words Chesnutt, after deftly explaining the racism behind southern white language on this topic, shows that Mississippi, Louisiana, Michigan, Ohio, and South Carolina all have different answers for this question.

The Far West

The West has always held a special place in the American imagination. Its importance was memorably put in the American consciousness by Frederick Jackson Turner in a famous paper, "The Significance of the Frontier in American History" (1893). Turner wrote, in part, "Up to our day, American history has been in large degree the history of the colonization of the Great West. The existence of an area of free land, its continuous recession, and the advance of American settlement westward, explain American development." Whatever objections can be raised to Turner's ideas, it is certainly true that the traditions of individuality and equality and freedom in general flourished on the frontier, and that the west after the Civil War was a more egalitarian, if coarser, society than that of the east. When social conditions became too oppressive in the east, an American in the nineteenth century could, like Huckleberry Finn, "light out for the territory ahead of the rest."

Some of the crudeness and homespun justice of the West, and of California in particular, comes through in Mark Twain's *Roughing It,* but the first to specialize in telling the story of those who journeyed westward was the short story writer and sometime poet Francis Bret Harte (1836–1902). Although he was born in Albany, New York, Harte migrated west shortly after the Gold Rush of 1849 and, like Mark Twain, he became a newspaperman, printing vignettes and stories in California newspapers. Harte's best writing was the first book composed from these efforts: *The Luck of Roaring Camp and Other Sketches* (1870).

"The Luck of Roaring Camp" is a baby remarkably born to a prostitute named Cherokee Sal. "Death was by no means uncommon in Roaring Camp, but a birth was a new thing." Cherokee Sal dies shortly after childbirth, but the baby, named at first Luck and then Tommy Luck, lives and is taken care of by a man named Stumpy, one of the "loungers" in Roaring Camp. The child's arrival changes the place. A collection is taken up, the level of swearing decreases, and the men collectively become doting parents. Stumpy becomes a protective, caring father. Then a snowy winter arrives. When the snow melts, the river overflows its banks and floods the town. Stumpy's cabin is washed away, Luck goes missing, and the men return to the settlement "with sad hearts." A relief boat arrives with the child in the arms of another settler; however, the boy is dead and the settler who has attempted to rescue him, dies too, saying, "Tell the boys I've got Luck with me now." It is a memorable, sad tale.

A second story, "The Outcasts of Poker Flat," has even more Californian scenery in it, ends as brutally, and is told with the same humor. "The Outcasts of Poker Flat" is centered on the figure of a gambler, John Oakhurst, who, with two prostitutes and an alcoholic "sluice-robber" (a man who steals gold from troughs others have set up to catch it as it washes through the river) is cast out of the town in the name of frontier justice. The four set out through the Sierra Mountains for the neighboring town of Sandy Bar. Part way on this arduous journey, they stop and meet up with a boy, Tom Simson, called "The Innocent," and his girlfriend. They too are running away from Sandy Bar. The scenery in the High Sierras is both awe inspiring and deadly; the characters, like those in Roaring Camp, prove ultimately worthy.

The Midwest

Of all the areas of the United States—New England, the South, the far West, and the Midwest—the Midwest has least been explored by local color writers. Except for Chicago, which was a publishing center (Kate Chopin's *The Awakening* appeared from a Chicago press in 1899), the Midwest has the fewest literary venues and is also geographically the largest. There are perhaps two well-known distinctly regional writers from the Midwest. The first, Edward Eggleston (1837–1902), has one book but half-remembered today, *The Hoosier Schoolmaster* (1871), a love story between an Indiana schoolmaster and a hired girl. A later novel, *The Circuit Rider* (1874) looks at the amoral ways of Ohio backwoods types and has a social message that came to dominate Eggleston's later production.

Hamlin Garland (1860–1940)

It is the work of Hamlin Garland that best captured the life of common people in the Midwest. Deeply aware of the unspoken social codes and traditions of that region, Garland produced one landmark

■ ■ ■ ■ THE RAILROAD ■ ■ ■ ■ ■

At the turn of the twentieth century, rail travel was one of the major means of covering long distances. In his novel about race riots, Charles Chesnutt makes use of the railroad as an emblem of segregation. Shelia Smith McKoy, in her study When Whites Riot, explains the force and associations of the railroad in Chesnutt's 1901 novel *The Marrow of Tradition*.

. . . the railroad has always been a symbol of America's racial schizophrenia. In African American literature, references to trains and the railroad recall the racial divide implicit in a variety of discourses on race. Railroads marked the dividing line between black and white America, from providing the line of demarcation between segregated communities to the existence of Jim Crow cars. The Jim Crow cars were the space in which Pullman porters found both economic opportunity and racial subjugation. They represented racial difference especially as it was shaped in the laws governing race between the North and the South. The rail system, in essence, was the marker of the differences between America's promise and its racial practices.

Throughout all of his writing Chesnutt is concerned with frontiers between the races and the mutability of these boundaries, the ways in which they are defined and shifted, and in their changes realign and reorganize interior and exterior lives.

work of fiction, the six stories in *Main-Travelled Roads* (1891), and several autobiographies, *Son of the Middle Border* (1917), *Daughter of the Middle Border* (1921), that indelibly etched a portrait of this region of the United States.

The fiction came first. Bitter, unindulgent, written with verve and freshness, the narratives express the harsh conditions of farm life in Wisconsin and the Dakotas. Some of them have their roots in Garland's own experience. He was born in poverty in the Midwest and moved east to Boston, where he became a successful writer, teacher, and lecturer. "Up the Coulé" illustrates his best qualities.

Howard McLane, a successful New York actor, returns home to his farm west of Milwaukee. Upon arriving, he is both exhilarated by the freshness and beauty of the landscape and struck by his own alienation from it.

Howard is both part of the landscape and its traditions ("Howard knew the Western man too well to press the matter of pay") and,

Bret Harte
Stick-pin and watch-fob elegant, Harte was the successful literary man. When he first came east, the story goes, he attended elegant receptions in his cowboy boots. Hostesses forgave him because he seemed to symbolize the West.

because he is now a New Yorker with elegant clothes and a high salary, not part of it. The character who dramatizes the difference is Howard's brother Grant. Grant has remained on the farm and worked it hard.

Along with Garland's sympathy for the plight of the farmer is a corresponding sense of the toll this life exacts upon farm wives. Grant's wife tells Howard, "I was a fool for ever marrying . . . I made a decent living teaching. I was free to come and go, my money was my own. Now I'm tied right down to a churn or a dishpan. I never have a cent of my own. *He's* growling 'round half the time, and there's no chance of his ever being different."

Clearly this story wants not only to give a sense of the beauty and futility of Midwestern farm life but also to introduce reform. Garland's solution to the plight of the farmer is a confiscatory tax or a "single tax" in which all the benefits of the work are returned to the community for its own benefit—a mandated SOCIALISM or equal sharing of assets.

The urge for social reform among regional American writers was widespread but, curiously, split along gender lines. Women local colorists tended to focus on the inner lives of the characters and find strength within; male writers saw situations more externally and edged toward social platforms. All of the local colorists worked before the first influx of writers of the progressive era—writers whose fiction was deeply tied up in more or less explicit reformist politics.

Willa Cather (1873–1947)

One of the best examples of a woman regionalist and perhaps the finest artist of this group—certainly the one with the most sustained output—was Willa Cather. She writes about two regions, the Midwest and the Southwest. Although she was born in Virginia, Cather moved to Nebraska when she was ten. Her most famous novels—*O Pioneers!* (1913), *The Song of the Lark* (1915), and *My Ántonia* (1918)— take place on the Great Plains, the Nebraska country, with its shifting immigrant population. Having written numerous short stories and a dozen novels, Cather lived until the middle of the twentieth century, at which point she herself was an ICON of the past that she increasingly valued.

My Ántonia, a story-within-a-story, is the tale of an insider: "no one who had not grown up in a little prairie town could know anything about it," the narrator explains. This nameless narrator introduces the manuscript of a fellow-midwesterner, Jim Burden, who in turn tells Ántonia's story. Ántonia Schimerda and Jim live in Black Hawk,

Willa Cather
Taken by Nikolas Muray in the 1920s, this photo of Cather shows her wearing a simple Indian-like jacket. Photographs of Cather are relatively scarce; she was a private person.

Nebraska. The Shimerdas, from Czechoslovakia, are naïve land purchasers. They buy a difficult parcel of land. Unlike the Burdens, they are not suited for farming. Mr. Shimerda, who is fragile, has an artistic temperament. He loves music. He craves the warm safety of the Burden household but is unable to establish such security for himself. Impractical and overcome by years of homesickness, Mr. Shimerda shoots himself.

That act leaves the Shimerdas destitute. Ántonia with her older brother works for a while on the Burdens' farm and becomes a maid when the Burdens move into town. Eventually she marries a railway conductor, but the marriage does not last, and he runs away, leaving their child with her. She works on her brother's farm, where Jim Burden, now a Harvard law student, visits. She is "thinner" and "worked down" and yet with "a new kind of strength in the gravity of her face." Ántonia is twenty-four.

Twenty years later Jim, now become a world traveler, receives a letter from Ántonia telling him that she has married a Bohemian named Anton Cuzak. They have many children and work on a large farm. Unlike Ántonia's father, this Bohemian is adaptable: "At first I near go crazy with lonesomeness . . . but my woman is got such a warm heart." Jim ends the story on a note of nostalgia, affirmation, and loneliness: "Whatever we [Jim and Ántonia] had missed [by being separated], we possessed together the precious, the incommunicable past."

Ántonia, whose struggles and loves Cather presents in both direct and reported forms, is an emblem of all that Willa Cather wished to affirm. Loving and energetic, Ántonia endures. She stands apart from the slick, manipulative world of commerce and "getting ahead." She is a strong woman. While there are many such in Cather's work—e. g., Alexandra Bergson in *O Pioneers!* and Thea Kronborg in *The Song of the Lark*—Cather, unlike Garland or Chesnutt, has no reformist (or feminist) agenda. She is apart from movements. The feeling of her work in these three novels is ELEGIAC.

This feeling came increasingly to characterize Cather's writing. The works that followed moved toward the Southwest, focusing on the human values that Cather felt the crass, modern world rejected: emotional courage, grace, charm, and a reverence for the beautiful. Her own prose deliberately exemplifies these traits. Increasingly, as Cather grew older, these were joined by a quiet religious sensibility.

This palpable nostalgia reaches its high point in three of Cather's later novels, *A Lost Lady* (1923), *The Professor's House* (1925),

▪ ▪ ▪ ▪ A STORM ▪ ▪ ▪ ▪

My Ántonia bounds in lyricism and precise description of life in the Midwest.

> *All the nights were close and hot during that harvest season. The harvesters slept in the hayloft because it was cooler there than in the house. I used to lie in my bed by the open window, watching the heat lightning play softly along the horizon, or looking up at the gaunt frame of the windmill against the blue night sky. One night there was a beautiful electric storm, though not enough rain fell to damage the cut grain. The men went down to the barn immediately after supper, and when the dishes were washed, Ántonia and I climbed up on the slanting roof of the chicken-house to watch the clouds. The thunder was loud and metallic, like the rattle of sheet iron, and the lightning broke in great zigzags across the heavens, making everything stand out and come close to us for a moment. Half the sky was chequered with black thunderheads, but all the west was luminous and clear: in the lightning flashes it looked like deep blue water, with the sheen of moonlight on it; and the mottled part of the sky was like marble pavement, like the quay of some splendid seacoast city, doomed to destruction. Great warm splashes of rain fell on our upturned faces. One black cloud, no bigger than a little boat, drifted out into the clear space unattended, and kept moving westward. All about us we could hear the felty beat of the raindrops on the soft dust of the farmyard. Grandmother came to the door and said it was late, and we would get wet out there.*

and *Death Comes for the Archbishop* (1927). All three as well as much of Cather's other work might be put under the EPIGRAPH or introductory saying which Cather attached to *My Ántonia* from the great Latin poet, Virgil: "Otima dies . . . prima fugit." The best days are the first to flee.

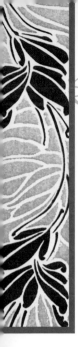

6. Naturalism, Determinism, Social Reform: Crane, Norris, London, DuBois, Sinclair, Dreiser

Many local colorists and regionalists are PROTEST WRITERS: they write to object to or expose a system (financial or social) that they feel is unfair and corrupt, one that benefits property owners, for example, at the expense of the workers. This objection was not unique to regionalists. It was part of the spirit of the end of the nineteenth century. Influenced by European biologists, philosophers, and physicists, the way writers understood the mechanics of life itself, on a grand scale, was changing.

One constant in this thinking was the idea that people were not free, that their destinies were controlled not by themselves but by their environment. A writer who follows NATURALISM aims, like a realist, to describe life as it is lived, without false, sentimental or contrived "happy" endings. Unlike realists, though, naturalists do not believe human beings can control what they do: they are not free. They may lament the harshness of life, but they feel powerless to alter it.

Pushed further, naturalism leads to DETERMINISM, the belief that every action and every thought of a person has been shaped by previous experience and the environment. Although Marxists may believe that eventually the tide of events will force change, philosophically determinism is at odds with social protest. How can a person hope to change anything if what happens is fated? Determinism also undercuts itself: if every thought has been determined, then the thoughts of the determinist have been too; determinism is not the objective stance it claims to be.

Stephen Crane (1871–1900)

For the first half of the twentieth century, Stephen Crane was considered the writer of *The Red Badge of Courage* (1895) and a few extraordinarily vivid short stories, "The Open Boat," "The Blue Hotel," and "The Bride Comes to Yellow Sky." Excitingly written, *The Red Badge of Courage* occurs during the Civil War, but only a few details—the colors of the soldiers' uniforms and bits of dialogue—indicate its historical setting. Crane is only incidentally interested in the particulars of the Civil War.

Crane's first book, self-published and written under the PSEUDONYM Johnston Smith, *Maggie, a Girl of the Streets* (1896), is a novel of urban despair. The daughter of a drunken, small-time

New York Tenement

There was a finite amount of land in large cities. Several poor families frequently lived in one small apartment. Aware of this practice, landlords often increased the rent. Here, washing is hung out to dry on a rickety, but typical, firetrap building.

■ ■ ■ ■ CRANE'S POETRY ■ ■ ■ ■

Stephen Crane was a highly original poet. Many of his short, apparently simple poems carry a heavy philosophical weight and are pithy statements of his beliefs.

> *A man said to the universe:*
> *"Sir, I exist!"*
> *"However," replied the universe,*
> *"That fact has not created in me*
> *A sense of obligation."*

This seemingly casual poem is subtler than it at first appears and is further testimony to Crane's deftness as a stylist. There is a deliberate contrast between the gravity of the dramatic situation—a man speaking to the universe itself!—and the brevity of the poem: five short lines. On further inspection, the brevity is appropriate since the topic of the poem is the lack of connection between humanity and the cosmos in which it finds itself; there is really nothing to be said, although given the protest of the first speaker, much is evidently felt.

The nobility of the man's declaration—three strongly accented syllables in a four syllable line—is deftly set off against the universe's bureaucratic, polysyllabic, dismissal. The effect is ironic and lightly comic, a mood intensified by the distance of the reader from the original speaker. Unlike in the case of Henry Fleming, the reader never gets to know the "man." The nature of the circumstances that prompted the original "Sir, I exist!" are never given, so the reader cannot identify any more with the man than the uninterested universe. It is, in effect, a poem reduced to its bare bones, the skeleton of human existence as Crane sees it.

criminal mother, Maggie is seduced by a friend of her brother. Jilted, she turns to prostitution and eventually commits suicide, trapped by the squalid alternatives of her life. This material and ambience came from Crane's hard experience growing up in New Jersey and New York.

Crane's turning toward a subject—war—that he had not yet experienced provided an imaginative impetus that set off his talents to greater effect. While adhering to the realism of *Maggie, The Red Badge of Courage* generalizes its account of "an episode of the Civil War" by zeroing in on the unremarkable moments that shape the lives of soldiers.

Probably based on the battle of Chancellorsville, the novel does not specify the location of the fighting. The main figure, a Union soldier named Henry Fleming, is rarely mentioned by name; instead he is called "the youth" or "he." The details of soldiering, however, are put down with brisk particularity: "Men extricated themselves from thick shirts. Presently few carried anything but their necessary clothing, blankets, haversacks, canteens, and arms and ammunition. 'You can now eat and shoot,' said the tall soldier to the youth. 'That's all you want to do.'"

The soldierly life is marked by confusion and purposelessness. After running "like a blind man" in battle, Fleming becomes appalled at his cowardice, a feeling that intensifies after he sees a friend die grotesquely: "For a moment the tremor of his legs caused him to dance a sort of hideous hornpipe. His arms beat wildly about his head in an expression of implike enthusiasm." Fleming may be tortured by guilt, but the world around him is supremely unconcerned. "As he gazed around him the youth felt a flash of astonishment at the blue, pure sky and the sun gleamings on the trees and fields. It was surprising that Nature had gone tranquilly on with her golden process in the midst of so much devilment."

Ironic ambiguities lie at the heart of the story. The central METAPHOR of the book, mentioned in the title, signifies a wound. The one Fleming receives is visited upon him, passively, as he is struggling in a retreat with one of his compatriots, not actively, in battle. "He saw the flaming wings of lightning flash before his vision. There was a deafening rumble of thunder within his head." No mention is made of the action directly; Crane encourages the reader to be as puzzled and unaware as the central character is. (In Ernest Hemingway's *A Farewell to Arms* [1929], Lieutenant Frederick Henry, whose name owes something to Henry Fleming, is wounded in the same way.)

This passivity extends to what occurs after the wounding. Fleming lets others believe that he has been wounded in battle. It is not an active deception. Fleming's acceptance as a full-time soldier gives him the feeling of belonging that he has needed, even though based on false pretenses.

Fleming becomes a legitimate hero in the same way, through accidents and unconscious actions. He is egged on by a lieutenant who says, before the Confederates attack again, "there's too much chin music and too little fightin' in this war. The youth was not conscious that he was erect upon his feet. He did not know the direction of the ground." He loads cartridges into his hot rifle and fires even after there is no enemy at which to shoot. The lieutenant "called out to the youth, 'By heavens, if I had ten thousand wildcats like you I could tear th' stomach outa this war in less'n a week!'"

The last chapters of *The Red Badge of Courage* describe a youth who has turned into a man without realizing what he was about.

The bumbling behind heroism is thrown into crisp relief by Crane's energetic, colorful style, with its famous metaphors—e. g., "The red sun was pasted in the sky like a wafer,"—with its realistic dialogue, full of slang and profanity daring for its day, and its sharp irony. Almost every chapter concludes with a brief, pithy sentence either contrasting the bloody action immediately previous to it or full of understated menace—for example, "We'll git swallowed." The vision of the Civil War in the most famous novel to come out of it has nothing to do with the causes for which it was fought.

Frank Norris (1870–1902)

Born in Chicago, Frank Norris moved to San Francisco at fourteen. After attending the University of California and Harvard University, he spent time as a newspaper correspondent. Encouraged in his literary efforts at Harvard, where part of his first successful book was written, Norris was an admirer of Émile Zola (1840–1902), a French writer who originated naturalism and disdained AESTHETICISM. He wanted only to tell the truth as he saw it. "I am little concerned with beauty of perfection," Zola wrote; "all I care about is life, struggle, intensity." Norris's own statements about writing echo these sentiments.

Because of their insistence on describing all aspects of life without filtering or idealizing any aspect of it, naturalists ran into trouble with censors. More shocking than the realistic descriptions of lower-class existence is a scene in Norris's first successful novel *McTeague* where the dentist, McTeague, etherizes Trina while she is sitting in his dental chair and then takes sexual advantage of her.

The inexorable forces of nature and the sweep of life seen on a grand scale are evident in Norris's masterpiece *The Octopus* (1902). In this great, vibrant, energetic grab-bag novel Norris's contradictory impulses operate closer to the surface than they do in *McTeague*. Multiple plots unfold simultaneously, all loosely bound together by the central image of the Octopus itself, an animal metaphor that stands for the force that dominates the lives of the characters and controls the economic life of the region. In *The Octopus*, Norris describes the railroad engine in horrific splendor: "the galloping monster, the terror of steel and steam, with its single eye, cyclopean, red, shooting from horizon to horizon . . . the symbol of a vast power, huge, terrible . . . the monster, the Colossus, the Octopus."

The most obvious conflict is that between the ranchers and the railroad. The opening chapters show that the railroad and its oily representative, S. Behrman, own the land the farmers need in order to earn their livelihood. The ranchers, determined to fight, are by turns anguished and sweet, callow and frustrated.

A second plot line involves the mystic Vanamee. A lonely outsider who sometimes works on the ranches, Vanamee has lost the love of his life, Angele, but he is friends with the lonely poet Presley, also an outsider, and is drawn to the church. In touch with spiritual forces outside the calculating world of the railroad and the more practical wheat farmers, he eventually achieves a spiritual reunion with Angele.

Just as *The Octopus* contains disparate elements, it contains disparate thoughts. No attentive reader can help being puzzled by contradictions in Norris's thinking. The early chapters and much of the middle section of the book condemn the evil of greed and the power of money. S. Behrman is a villain out of old-time melodramas—from his hypocritical geniality, his ruthlessness, down to his fat, sweaty neck. (*The Octopus* exudes racism: the good farmers are blond Nordics; Behrman is Jewish.) The position seems clear: evil must be resisted, even at the price of self-destruction, as in the case of Dyke.

Evil? How can naturalism make such a judgment? In fact *The Octopus* openly admits this contradiction. In Book II, Presley, now famous for his socialist poem "The Toilers," is granted an interview with S. Behrman's boss, head of the railroad, Shelgrim. Instead of finding a more devious, smoother Behrman, Presley encounters a soft-hearted, sentimental employer who forgives the alcoholism of one of his employees and who explains, with tired condescension, that he himself is the in the grip of forces beyond his power. "I can *not* control [the railroad]. It is a force born out of certain conditions, and I—no man—can stop it or control it." This exciting scene muddies the waters. If the chief executive cannot master the railroad, what can the efforts of lesser men do? Clearly *The Octopus* is the product of an excitingly talented writer but not of a cool-headed thinker.

> ■ ■ ON FRANK NORRIS ■ ■
>
> *The key to Norris's mind is to be found in a naïve, open-hearted, and essentially unquenchable joy as radiant as the lyricism of Elizabethan poetry, a joy that is like the first discovery of the world, exhilarating in its directness, and eager to absorb every flicker of life.*
>
> –Alfred Kazin, *On Native Grounds*
>
> No one who reads Norris's fiction can miss the aptness of Alfred Kazin's appreciation. The reader is left agreeably breathless; no other serious novel until the *U.S.A.* trilogy by John Dos Passos offers such exhilaration. *The Octopus* sweeps along, incident after sensational incident, each seeming to outdo the previous. Its broadness of scope, its eagerness to engage all elements of western life dramatize the boundlessness of the West, the vision and aspiration that drove Americans to settle an untamed country, and the fecundity of that country. Nothing is outside this novel's scope; it is exhausting and exhaustive.

Jack London (1876–1916)

Readers familiar today with the name of Jack London may be unaware of his colorful, knockabout life. Like Norris, London was a Californian. His father was probably an astrologer named W. H. Chaney, and his teenage years were spent among stevedores and waterfront workers. These influences shaped a man careless of his health, who drank and lived irregularly and who used and abused his talents. He never settled down, following the rush for gold in the Klondike in 1897, for example, setting off for the South Seas ten years later, and marrying twice before his death—almost certainly a suicide—at the age of forty.

It is remarkable in these circumstances that London achieved so much and read as widely as he did—and even more remarkable that he did it all on his own. He was self-taught. Unlike Frank Norris, London was a student of the work of the English biologist Charles Darwin, whose *Origin of the Species* (1859) set forth the theory of natural selection. Darwin explained that among animal groups, the strong succeed but the weak die out. Applied to human society, this idea is called SOCIAL DARWINISM. London also studied the German philosopher Frederich Nietzsche who glorified the ideal of the strong man, the ÜBERMENSCH or superman, a superior being to whom conventional notions of good and evil did not apply.

At the same time, however, London was a devotee of Karl Marx, whose *Das Kapital* (1873) proposed the idea of a Communist or socialist state. London believed that humanity would progress only if it adopted Marx's ideals. This idea conflicts with Social Darwinism. If all people work for the common good, the weak as well as the strong benefit.

Nearly a century after his death, many readers know London for his novel of the American Yukon *The Call of the Wild* (1903).

■ ■ BIERCE ON LONDON ■ ■

Ambrose Bierce, Jack London's contemporary, wrote of Wolf Larsen,

It doesn't really matter how London has hammered him into you. You may quarrel with the methods, but the result is almost incomparable. The hewing out and setting up of such a figure is enough for a man to do in one life-time.

There is something endearing about the work of Jack London notwithstanding its unevenness and its brashness. London might be a careless writer, may seem confused when he makes the types of people he wants to criticize more attractive than the types he wants to affirm, and is certainly a sentimentalist, but throughout all of his major works, one feels life being lived as though it mattered passionately. There are moments of despair and anguish—especially in *Martin Eden*—but London never gives up or goes for the small moment. He would rather lose on a grand scale than play it safe.

This novel proceeds from London's experiences in Alaska—which also provided material for his collection of short stories *The Son of the Wolf* (1900) within which is his best-known short story "To Build a Fire," about a man who eventually succumbs to the cold and, in a sense, submits to the superior elements—a form of suicide.

The thin line between civilized comportment and brute force also marks London's novel of 1904, *The Sea-Wolf*. The main conflict is between the POETASTER—a would-be poet—Humphrey Van-Weyden, the narrator, and the captain, Wolf Larsen, of the ship *The Ghost,* who gives the book its title. London's plot, however, seems to want to make VanWeyden the hero. VanWeyden in the course of the narrative saves the ship, organizes the crew, acts in a socially responsible way, and wins the love of the heroine, Maud Brewster.

The inner conflict and self-defeating nature of London are most clearly revealed in his autobiographical novel *Martin Eden* (1909). One of Eden's books, *The Shame of the Sun* (the narrative's obvious equivalent to *The Call of the Wild*), makes Eden wealthy and famous. As a consequence, a former girlfriend attempts to renew her engagement to him. Eden is repelled. Then a friend commits suicide. Eden, his socialist ideals useless in a personal crisis, finds life without direction or significance.

As would his creator half a dozen years later, Martin Eden ends his own life.

W. E. B. DuBois (1868–1965)

Imaginative fiction was one vehicle by which social thinkers sought to effect change in American life. Much of this fiction was written by white men who tried to reach out by including in their work immigrants and non-Americans, for example, the Hoovens, Wolf Larsen, the families discussed in the work of Sinclair and Dreiser below, and even—although there are no social programs implied in her fiction—the Shimerdas and Cusaks in Willa Cather's *My Ántonia.*

However, throughout the twentieth century, Americans continued to struggle with the issue of race relations. The Civil War turned into the fight for Civil Rights, and a central figure in the struggle for equality was W. E. B. DuBois, from Massachusetts. DuBois was a brilliant writer and thinker, a graduate of Harvard, who lived long enough to see the beginning of the Civil Rights Era. His major work, and a distinctly different perspective on race relations, comes in *The Souls of Black Folk* (1903).

For DuBois Americans have not solved the problem of how black people are treated by simply granting freedoms. Americans have not accorded black people the freedom to be themselves.

DuBois felt that the black leader Booker T. Washington and his followers had betrayed America itself because they were content to work within the freedoms granted by whites. He called for nothing less than a change in consciousness if America were to honor its own ideals of equality and justice.

Strikingly and evocatively, in the last, quite different chapter of *The Souls of Black Folk,* DuBois offers praise to "the Negro folk song." It is an emotional conclusion to an argument, a granting of perspective on DuBois's own thinking that both harks back to Douglass's analysis of the music of slaves and expresses the yearning for a world beyond the present that informed DuBois's life.

That life turned increasingly toward the same Communist or socialist ideals of progressive thinkers around the turn of the nineteenth and twentieth centuries. Whatever particular instance ignited the thoughts of social writers and thinkers, SOCIALISM, one of the most powerful ideas ever propounded, seemed to be if not always the end then at least a stopping point along the way. Socialism is an economic system in which there is no private property.

Muckraking and Sinclair's *The Jungle*

Both Norris and London flirted with if they did not wholly commit themselves to socialist philosophies. Around 1900 many writers did exactly that. The rich were much richer than they had ever been. Immigration swelled the numbers of poor people who were crowded into unhealthy, unsanitary urban environments. Children were forced to work to help support their families. Many writers, artists, and thinkers wished to reform the laws that permitted these abuses. They called themselves PROGRESSIVES.

There had always been centers for assisting the poor— reformer Jane Addams' Hull House was one; writers of fiction, however, can act obliquely, not directly like Jane Addams. They expose conditions so that the general outcry forces change. Journalists who act in this way are called MUCKRAKERS. They rake up "muck" for all to see. Ida Tarbell (1857–1944) was one of the most famous muckrakers in her time; her articles about Rockefeller's Standard Oil Company, now called Exxon, resulted in a change of banking laws and the breaking up of TRUSTS. Similarly, the muckraking photographer Jacob Riis (1849–1914) depicted slum conditions in his memorably titled *How the Other Half Lives* (1890).

One often hears that literature can "make a difference" in people's lives. Proponents of the power of literature to effect change do not mean the gradual education of a reader; they intend something

▪ ▪ ▪ ▪ How a Sausage Is Made ▪ ▪ ▪ ▪

Theodore Roosevelt was not much taken with socialism, yet even he responded to Upton Sinclair's description of the storage of sausage meat in *The Jungle*. That book caused a revolution in the meat-packing industry. This is the description of that practice, followed by extracts from Roosevelt's vigorous letter to Sinclair:

> *There would be meat stored in great piles in rooms; and the water from the leaky roofs would drip over it, and thousands of rats would race about on it. It was too dark in these storage places to see well, but a man could run his hand over these piles of meat and sweep off handfuls of dried dung of rats. These rats were nuisances, and the packers would put poisoned bread out for them; they would die, and then rats, bread, and meat would go into the hoppers together. This is no fairy story and no joke; the meat would be shoveled into carts, and then men who did the shoveling would not take the trouble to lift out a rat when they saw one— there were things that went into the sausage in comparison with which a rat was a tidbit.*

In March 1906, Roosevelt writes to Sinclair, "I have now read, if not all, yet a good deal of your book, and if you come down here during the first week in April I shall be particularly glad to see you."

Roosevelt goes on to discuss the brand of socialism Sinclair advocates in his novel and adds, "Personally I think that one of the chief early effects of such attempts to put socialism of the kind there preached into practice, would be the elimination by starvation, and the diseases, moral and physical, attendant upon starvation, of that same portion of the community on whose behalf socialism would be invoked.

. . . But all this has nothing to do with the fact that the specific evils you point out shall, if their existence be proved, and if I have power, be eradicated."

more direct. They imply that the effects of progressive literature are immediate and evident. The one book that advocates of "the power of literature to bring about change" most often point to is a 1906 novel by Upton Sinclair (1878–1968), *The Jungle*.

The novel is the story of an immigrant, Jurgis Rudkus, married to Ona Lukoszaite, who seeks a job in the Chicago stockyards. Living in poverty, with real estate sharpies and his bosses taking advantage of him, he secures a position in a sausage–making plant. Hinting at what is to come, Sinclair writes that Jurgis accepts this work immediately after a child in the story has died possibly from "the smoked sausage he had eaten that morning—which may have been made out of some tubercular pork that was condemned as unfit for export."

Sinclair wrote for the moment with a deeper artistry than any of the muckrakers or dabblers in socialism possessed. Another writer of such abilities, with extensive powers of empathy, existed: Theodore Dreiser.

Theodore Dreiser (1871–1945)

Like Hamlin Garland, Theodore Dreiser was a son of the Midwest. Born in Terre Haute, Indiana, into a rural poverty not unlike that described in *Main-Travelled Roads,* Dreiser was early on attracted to the dandyism some of his characters affect. Possessed of a lumbering, sometimes heavy-handed and crude style, Dreiser soaked up details of city life, of how people-on-the-make achieve

■ ■ ■ ■ Assessments of Dreiser ■ ■ ■ ■

Dreiser, more than any other man, marching alone, usually unappreciated, often hated, has cleared the trail from Victorian and Howellsian timidity and gentility in American fiction to honesty and boldness and passion of life.

So said Sinclair Lewis, in his Nobel Prize address. Whether this praise was an attempt to flatter Dreiser or not is unclear, for Dreiser was the American most in contention in 1930, the year that Lewis was awarded the prize.

What is meant by this comparison is that at his worst Dreiser is a very clumsy writer. Here is a sentence from *The Financier* that should have been revised: "What was amiss, therefore, with himself and Stener and with Cowperwood as their—or rather Stener's secret representative, since Strobik did not dare to appear in the matter—buying now sufficient street—railway shares in some one line to control it, and then, if he, Strobik, could by efforts of his own, get the city council to set aside certain streets for its extension, why, there you were—they would own it."

This is stylistically awful. However, it is only one sentence in a book whose knowledge of finance, social relations, love, politics, and the connections between all them, make a comprehensive portrait of business life. Lewis was right: Dreiser cleared the way, and it was a Herculean task.

▪ ▪ ▪ ▪ AMERICAN LIFE IN 1900 ▪ ▪ ▪ ▪

Population of the United States	76,094,000
Living in cities of 2500 or more	30,160,000
Living in the country	45,835,000
White	56,595,000
Foreign born white	10,214,000
Black	8,834,000
American Indian	237,000
Asian born	114,000
Average life expectancy (M)	46.3 years
Average life expectancy (F)	48.3 years
Working Men	29,030,000
Working Women	5,319,000
Total deaths from motor vehicles	under 100
Total lynchings	115

The first fact likely to strike any peruser of the above table is the short life expectancy for both women and men. Even if the figures are skewed by unusually high childbirth mortality, the expected lifetime for men and women was still quite short. Many diseases that we now take for granted as curable such as smallpox, tuberculosis, and syphilis were killers at the start of the 20th century.

The proportion of African Americans and other races was much lower in relation to the number of whites living in America, while the number of lynchings actually exceeded the number of deaths from automobile accidents.

America was a more rural country in 1900. Writers such as Hamlin Garland who were writing about life on the farm were talking about more Americans than writers about such a subject would be today. America was still a small town country.

success, of how fancy bars and hotel businesses work, how sports take a place in American life, how people live in the slums and in moneyed resorts, of the way commerce operates, and how people high and low seduce, love, and betray. Unlike the more judgmental Norris, London, and Sinclair, Dreiser holds back. He explains what people do and what forces make them do it. Over the course of his long novels, his precision and even-handedness accumulate until his presentations crystallize into a complete picture.

Taken as a whole, Dreiser's fiction constitutes an authoritative report on the financial and social doings of America in the first two and a half decades of the twentieth century. Every class, from the highest to the lowest, finds its way into his pages: the dogged, the lucky, the out-of-luck, immigrants, artists, businessmen, the ordinary, the wealthy, and the impoverished.

His first novel, *Sister Carrie* (1900), endorsed by Frank Norris, caused a scandal when it was published, although it seems tame now. Carrie Meeber, a working-class girl, arrives in Chicago to stay with her sister and brother-in-law. She secures a numbing factory job that does not pay well. Her brother-in-law is unsympathetic. Instead of staying with her sister and family, she becomes the mistress of a salesman named Drouet. She acts in amateur theatricals. Shallow and opportunistic, Drouet introduces her to his friend, George Hurstwood, an unhappily married restaurant manager.

Finding him more appealing and of higher class than Drouet, Carrie runs away with him, first to Canada, then to New York. To finance his new life, Hurstwood has stolen $10,000 from the safe of the saloon where he works. But he is unable to establish himself at the same level as in Chicago. He goes into decline. Meanwhile, to support the two of them Carrie obtains work as a chorus girl and moves through a series of lesser parts until she becomes a well-known actress.

Sister Carrie has no social message, and Dreiser went on to compose additional novels that explore the areas *Sister Carrie* began to look at. In his "Trilogy of Desire," *The Financier* (1912), *The Titan* (1914), and *The Stoic* (1947, published posthumously), Dreiser explores the world of Frank Algernon Cowperwood, a financial wheeler-dealer.

Throughout his life Dreiser was preoccupied with social mechanisms, with the interplay of will and chance. His most famous book is the two-volume (in its original edition) novel *An American Tragedy* (1925). Here the social canvas is wider than in *Sister Carrie*, and although the essential outlines of his hero are similar to those of Carrie, Clyde Griffiths is more tightly bound to his fate. The murder of his girlfriend Roberta while he is in a rowboat is an event that happens to him more than something that comes as a result of his active agency.

Life may consist of chance meetings of will and fate, but the legal system will not accept such ambiguities. After a lengthy trial, Clyde Griffiths is condemned to death: an American tragedy.

Dreiser's presentation of American society influenced the writers of the 1920s. H. L. Mencken, Sinclair Lewis, and even F. Scott Fitzgerald were all impressed, if not with Dreiser's style, then with his human understanding and the largeness of his vision, an appropriate climax to the age of realism.

7. Other African American Voices

Until the passage of the Thirteenth Amendment to the Constitution (1865), which outlawed slavery in the United States, few African Americans had the opportunity or the encouragement to pursue a literary vocation. A chosen few, such as Phillis Wheatley, were published through the largesse of white patrons, a source of support that also helped launch the careers of famous ABOLITIONISTS such as Frederick Douglass and Harriet Jacobs, whose works are discussed in Chapter Two. However, until a literate audience could be established for its literature, the African American imagination would express itself primarily through an oral tradition—the preaching of sermons, the singing of spirituals, and the telling of folk tales.

Of the 4.5 million African Americans living in the United States by 1860, 4 million of them were enslaved and forbidden by law to learn to read and write. Many writers, including Douglass, commented on the relationship between literacy and the desire for freedom. Douglass maintained that learning to read sparked the desire for freedom in many slaves. His view is confirmed by one study that found that 20 percent of all the runaway slaves in Kentucky were literate while only 5 percent of all slaves could read. Therefore, a literate slave was four times more likely to run away. Clearly, slave owners were aware of this fact, which helps to explain why there were tough penalties for teaching slaves to read. African Americans associated reading with liberation and economic advantage, and, in the years following the Emancipation, the number of literate African Americans soared.

This lack of African American voices leaves a significant gap in American history and literature. Although these millions of people played a vitally important role in American life and society, little of what they thought and felt is reflected in most studies of American literature and culture. There were undoubtedly, in Thomas Gray's words, thousands of "mute, inglorious Milton[s]," people with the genius to write but who lacked the education and opportunity. Moreover, what writing exists from the period up to the Emancipation often reflects white ideas and values. In fact, white abolitionists controlled most of the means of publication for works written by African Americans, and all published works by former slaves were either heavily edited or dictated to abolitionists. No matter how well-intentioned these white abolitionist writers and editors were, they were ultimately more concerned that these works be *believable* than accurate or truthful representations of slave life. The goal of most abolitionists was to publish works that outraged northerners, thereby motivating them to oppose vigorously the institution of slavery.

The Narrative of James Williams (1838)

Unfortunately, one of the earliest published slave narratives, *The Narrative of James Williams*, which was dictated to the Quaker poet and anti-slavery activist John Greenleaf Whittier, proved to be less than completely reliable. Early advertisements for the work proclaimed that "the perfect accordance of his [Williams's] statements (made at different times to different individuals) one with one another, as well as those statements themselves, all afford strong confirmation of the truth and accuracy of his story." However, after the work's publication, it was revealed that Williams may have dictated his story in exchange for passage to England. Next, an editor from Alabama, J. B. Rittenhouse, went to work to disprove many of the so-called facts with which Williams had peppered his story. Abolitionists fired back that Williams had to disguise some names and places for his own safety. Each side pursued the argument for many months, and staunch abolitionists were not deterred in their belief in the emotional truth of Williams' story. Still, as abolitionist Lydia Maria Child wrote to a friend in December 1838, "[To] you and I, who look on the foundations upon which slavery rests, it is not the slightest consequence whether James Williams told the truth or not; yet the doubt thrown on his narrative is doing incalculable mischief." Intended to rouse white northerners to action, the FIASCO led some to give more weight to the southern position that slavery was a benign system run by honorable men and to doubt the tales of cruelty and humiliation that Williams told.

From this point forward, abolitionist publishers were especially careful to ensure that the stories they published were entirely factual, which was no doubt a good thing; however, they also edited with an eye to what white audiences would believe as well as an eye to making sure the audiences were suitably angered by what they read. Thus, whereas factual, many of the published works by slaves were mediated by white abolitionists' perspectives and goals, leading to the omission of certain facts and foregrounding others. Even Douglass, a formidable orator, was often coached. In his early years on the lecture circuit, the abolitionist John Collins told Douglass to "give us the facts and we will take care of the philosophy."

Thus, because it is difficult to get to the truth of the African American slave experience, and because so little was written down or compiled in any systematic way, works that attempt to discuss pre-Emancipation American literature and culture have had to rely on what was published, with the knowledge that the whole story lay somewhere in the background, silenced by both the system and the circumstances.

Literary Detective Work and the First Novel by an African American Woman

Fortunately, in the last several years, works have come into prominence that shed some light on unfiltered, or unmediated, African American views of slavery and the Civil War. There has been a good deal written about African American soldiers in the Civil War, but little has been told about those who were not combatants. In 2002, however, the eminent scholar of African American literature, Henry Louis Gates, Jr., published what may be the first novel ever written by an African American woman, someone who experienced life as a slave and ran away to settle in the free North. The semi-autobiographical novel was published as *The Bondwoman's Narrative* (2002), but the full title on the manuscript gives more information about the nature of the work: *The Bondwoman's Narrative by Hannah Crafts, a Fugitive Slave, Recently Escaped from North Carolina*. Whereas there is still some argument about who the writer was (Hannah Crafts appears to have been a PSEUDONYM), most experts agree that she was African American and wrote the novel between 1857 and 1860. It is thought that the novel had to have been completed before the outbreak of the Civil War in 1861, because the novel does not mention the event. Furthermore, there is a good deal of internal evidence that would indicate the novel could not have been written before 1857.

Like the earlier abolitionist publishers, Gates went to great lengths to AUTHENTICATE the manuscript and to try to discover who the real writer was. With modern technology and the help of several experts, he was able to determine that the manuscript was authentic, in the sense that it was written during the time of slavery. The paper, ink, kind of pen, and even the style of handwriting confirm that the book was not a recent forgery. Then Gates went to work to find out who Crafts might have been. She provides many clues in the manuscript, including the names of her owners

■ ■ THE SECOND NOVEL BY AN AFRICAN AMERICAN WOMAN ■ ■
Before Professor Gates discovered *The Bondwoman's Narrative*, he had
been instrumental in reviving interest in Harriet Wilson's *Our Nig: Or
Sketches from the Life of a Free Black*, an 1859 work that was thought to be
the first novel written by an African American woman. Like *The Bondwoman's Narrative, Our Nig* straddles two genres: that of the slave narrative and that of the nineteenth-century sentimental novel. Gates
influenced the novel's reissue in 1983 and revealed that its author was
an African American woman from Milford, New Hampshire. At the end
of the novel, Wilson steps out of her role as author and adds a plea to
the reading public to buy her book so she can earn enough to support
her son George. Gates was able to use this biographical information to
determine that young George Wilson died in 1860. Unfortunately, after
that date, Gates was unable to find any additional information about
Wilson.

Gates speculated—it turns out correctly—that *Our Nig* was at least partly
autobiographical. The novel tells the story of Frado, a six-year-old girl of
mixed parentage, whose white mother abandoned her when the girl's father
died. She was left with a white family on a farm in New Hampshire, not as
a slave, but as an indentured servant. Wilson's portrayal of Frado's treatment by her mistress, Mrs. Bellmont, is shocking; she was both physically
and mentally abused. At the age of 18, Frado's term of servitude is over.

and where she ultimately settled. Nevertheless, Gates has been
unable to pinpoint Crafts' identity to date. He and many other
scholars believe firmly that she was not white, although she was
clearly literate and very well read and, thus, one of the few literate African American slaves. Scholars have used internal evidence
from the novel, including how the author presents and identifies
both African American and white characters, to support this conclusion. Whereas white writers, Gates notes, typically use white
as the *default* (that is, you can assume a character is white unless otherwise described as black), Crafts tends not to portray her
characters in this fashion, labeling both races, and she seems to
be particularly attuned to the variety of *hues* in the black enslaved
population. In other words, she refers to those like herself whose
complexions are nearly white, to those who are "ebony," and to
everything in between.

She leaves the Bellmont household and works as a servant and seamstress until 1851 when she marries Thomas Wilson. Wilson abandons her while she is pregnant with their son, George.

Despite his best efforts, Gates was unable to learn anything about Harriet Wilson after 1860. In 1993, however, scholar Barbara White identified the family known in the novel as the Bellmonts to be Nehemiah Hayward, Jr., and his wife, Rebecca.

In the introduction to the 2005 Penguin edition of *Our Nig*, scholars Gabrielle Foreman and Reginald Pitts shared their research on Wilson and were able to illuminate significant portions of her life. It turns out she was born Harriet Adams in 1825. Her father was Joshua Green, a free African American, and her mother was Mag Smith, an Irish washerwoman. After 1860, Wilson turns up in Boston as a medium. In 1867, the Spiritualist newspaper *The Banner of Light* describes Wilson as an "eloquent and earnest colored trance medium." She remarried a white spiritualist—who was 18 years younger than she—John Gallatin Robinson, in 1870. The couple lived together until 1877, when they took up separate residences.

Wilson was a frequent lecturer at spiritualist meetings all over New England. She was also employed as a housekeeper. She died in Quincy, Massachusetts, in 1900. *Our Nig* is her only published work.

Scholars have also used both internal and external evidence to demonstrate that Crafts was, in fact, a woman and not a man writing in a woman's voice. The novel falls squarely in the DOMESTIC or SENTIMENTAL literary tradition, in which women and women's work are central to the story (as does *A Bondwoman's Narrative*), but works in this tradition were nearly all written by women. Moreover, whoever wrote *A Bondwoman's Narrative* sewed the pages together and used a thimble to form a seal on bits of paper pasted in the manuscript on which she made corrections—material forms that suggest female authorship.

As for whether Crafts was actually a runaway slave, there is much disagreement. Gates believes that she was and amasses a good deal of what might be called circumstantial evidence to prove his contention, including the author's use of the names of a real slaveholding couple, John Wheeler and his wife, Ellen, many geographical references, and what appears to be a realistic portrait of slave life, albeit the life of a fairly well-treated house slave. Other scholars question Gates' theory and suggest that Crafts may have been a free African American woman, perhaps a schoolteacher, who wrote her novel as a teaching device. Many teachers of the day did this and read their stories to their female students during sewing hour. Scholars who doubt that Crafts was ever a slave use inconsistencies in the dates when Crafts implies she was enslaved by the Wheelers and living with them in Washington, D.C. to question her actual status as a slave. However, those who do not believe she was a slave do not question the accuracy of her portrayal of slave life, believing that she was in a position to hear firsthand the stories of hundreds of fugitive slaves. These scholars who doubt Crafts regard her work as purely a novel, an invented story, rather than as a fictionalized autobiography.

More Detective Work

At least one scholar, Katherine E. Flynn, believes she has identified a fugitive slave who may have written the novel. The slave owners identified in *The Bondwoman's Narrative*, the Wheelers, were parties in a sensational case involving a runaway slave, known as Jane Johnson. In 1855, John Wheeler brought Johnson and her two sons with him to Philadelphia on a visit to his father-in-law, the painter Thomas Sully. While there, Johnson asked local abolitionists for help in gaining her freedom. By the time the abolitionists got to the hotel where Wheeler and his party were staying, they had already boarded a steamer for points south Passmore Williamson, a prominent abolitionist, boarded the steamer and told Johnson that under Pennsylvania law she was free to leave. She and both her sons left the boat and immediately went into hiding. Wheeler sued Williamson, claiming that he had taken the slaves against their wills. Williamson was jailed because he had violated the Fugitive Slave Act of 1850. Johnson, despite the very real possibility of her being captured and returned to slavery, showed up at Williamson's trial and testified on his behalf. She then disappeared again. Williamson served three months in jail, and his story was much published and discussed in abolitionist circles. [highly is not acceptable here as a synonym for much]

Flynn, as a result of a good deal of detective work, was able to trace much of the subsequent life of Johnson and puts forward her name as the real "Hannah Crafts." She makes an interesting case, but other scholars point out that Johnson was illiterate when

Henry Louis Gates, Jr. on *Our Nig*

In 2004, Harvard professor Henry Louis Gates, Jr. delivered a speech about African American writer Harriet E. Wilson at Milford Town Hall in Milford, New Hampshire. Gates is seen explaining to the audience some of the difficulties that arise when working with early manuscript such as Wilson's novel, *Our Nig*. After rediscovering the novel, Gates saw that it was republished in 1983. *Our Nig* is the earliest American work of fiction written by a black woman.

she escaped. Flynn notes, however, that an 1860 CENSUS indicates that Johnson, at least by that time, was literate. Still, if Johnson were illiterate at the time of her escape, it would have been nearly impossible to gain the degree of literacy that Crafts displays in that short amount of time; judging by the ALLUSIONS and literary references in *The Bondwoman's Tale*, the real Crafts read widely in both contemporary literature and the classics.

Joe Nickell, the primary authenticator of the manuscript, doubts that Johnson was the author because the manuscript MALIGNS her. One of the novel's characters, Mrs. Henry, *contrasts* Hannah and Jane, saying, "Hannah is a good girl; she has good principles, and is I believe a consistent Christian. I don't think your Jane was either." Nickell says, "I doubt that this attack on Jane Johnson's character would be one that the real Jane would advance publicly herself—not for novelistic purposes such as VERISIMILITUDE, not as a clever ploy to disguise her true identity; nor indeed for any rationale I can imagine."

Certainly, if Crafts had been a slave and, in fact, had escaped, her fictionalized account might be of more interest to scholars. However, even if the work were written by a free woman who learned about slavery and escape from others, the novel is still worthy of study as the first novel by an African American woman.

The Bondwoman's Narrative (2002)

It is important to note that *The Bondwoman's Narrative* is not a great work of literature. Its prose and many of its plot devices are borrowed, sometimes with little EMENDATION, from other works, including Charlotte Brontë's *Jane Eyre* (1847), Charles Dickens' *Bleak House* (1853), and Harriet Beecher Stowe's *Uncle Tom's Cabin* (1852). The novel is an odd combination of different narrative genres, including slave narrative, satire, sentimental or domestic literature, fairy tale, and gothic, sometimes moving from one to another in a rather jarring manner. Nevertheless, it is worth serious study for several reasons beyond the fact that it is a *first*. Crafts' prose is often excellent, and her character, viewpoint, and behavior all contribute to a greater understanding of the African American experience, both during and after slavery.

Crafts tells her story in the first person. She describes herself as nearly white in appearance and as someone who, though deprived of freedom, worked in relative comfort as a house slave. She shares many characteristics with Brontë's character, Jane Eyre, including the fact that she is an orphan (she never knew her mother)

Uncle Tom's Cabin
This poster for Harriet Beecher Stow's Uncle Tom's Cabin, printed at around the turn of the twentieth century, features a portrait of Stowe herself in the upper left corner and a large portrait of the Great Emancipator, Abraham Lincoln, in the lower right-hand corner. Surrounding the Lincoln portrait are characters from the novel, including Little Eva, Topsy, Simon Legree, and Uncle Tom himself.

■ ■ ■ ■ Aɴᴏᴛʜᴇʀ Cᴏʟᴏʀ Lɪɴᴇ ■ ■ ■ ■

One of the powerful slogans of the 1960s was "Black is Beautiful." Although the phrase was first used in a speech by abolitionist John Sweat Rock in 1858, it became the mantra of a movement in the 1960s and 1970s to encourage African Americans to appreciate their own racial characteristics. One of the saddest legacies of slavery in America is that many blacks felt that lighter skin tones, straight hair, thin lips, and small noses were more attractive than dark skin, kinky hair, and African features. Not only did white Americans discriminate against blacks, but blacks themselves also discriminated against one another based on these superficial qualities. In the early years of the twentieth century, some African American organizations actually did not allow a person to join if their skin was darker than a typical grocery bag. This legacy of slavery caused many African Americans to internalize the biases of their masters and to pass those biases on to their children without fully realizing the psychological damage—the self-hatred—that resulted. The Black Power Movement of the 1960s urged blacks to celebrate their appearance; as a result, the hairstyle known as the Afro became popular as many stopped straightening their hair.

This discrimination based on skin tone is a significant theme in *The Bondwoman's Narrative.* Hannah frequently comments on skin tone and seems to associate positive characteristics with light skin and negative characteristics with dark skin. So important during times of slavery were these distinctions that slaves and masters devised a system of labeling people by how much

and lives as a tenuous guest in her master's house. Like Jane, she takes refuge in reading, although, unlike Jane, she was taught in secret by an elderly white couple, Aunt Hetty and Uncle Siah, who are sent to jail for their efforts. As does Jane, she hides herself on a window seat behind heavy curtains in order to read without being bothered, and she describes herself as "shy and reserved," having "a silent unobtrusive way of observing things and events, and wishing to understand them better than I could.

It is while hiding behind curtains in the library at her master's plantation, Lindendale, that Hannah learns a secret that she has already intuited: her mistress is *passing,* or pretending to be white, even though she is actually African American. It turns out that years

African blood they were supposed to have. A person who had one white and one black parent and whose skin was often lighter than a person with no white blood was known as a *mulatto*. The word *quadroon* generally refers to a person who has three white grandparents (three-quarters white), the child of a union between a mulatto and a white person. Other terms that were used less frequently were *octoroon* (a person with seven white and one black grandparent) and even *quintroon* (the child of an octoroon and a white parent). Many mixed-race individuals looked white, and some "passed"—that is, they pretended to be white, even though they had black ancestors. This was an issue during slavery because of something known as the "one-drop" rule. Technically, a person with even one drop of African blood was considered black. Moreover, the children of enslaved mothers were considered slaves, and many white masters enslaved their own children with slave mistresses.

As late as 1896, the U.S. Supreme Court upheld the basis of segregation through its ruling in the case of *Plessy v. Ferguson*. The case began when Homer Plessy, a person who had seven white and one black grandparent, decided to protest segregation by sitting in the "whites-only" car of the East Louisiana Railroad. He was arrested and jailed. Plessy fought his arrest, and the case eventually ended up in the Supreme Court. The justices upheld the right of a state to make laws segregating whites and blacks. From this case emerged the concept of "separate but equal" that held for nearly 50 years. The justices ruled that separate facilities were not illegal as long as they were of the same quality.

earlier her mother switched her with the dead baby of the plantation's mistress, and she was raised without knowing about the switch until she was about to be married. At this point, the villain of the tale, a lawyer with the Dickensian name of Mr. Trappe, shows her proof that she is African American. After her marriage, he threatens to betray her to her husband. This event sets the novel's plot in motion. Hannah tells her mistress that she has overheard Trappe's threat and decrees that she must run away. Her mistress begs Hannah to accompany her, and Hannah assents. One of the most interesting elements in the novel is Hannah's reluctance to escape merely to save her own skin. Again, like Jane, she subordinates herself to an orthodox scheme of Christian values, and she is staunch in her adherence to those values. Despite the fact that she recognizes slavery as evil, she also refuses to repay evil with evil and will not lie to save herself.

The Theme of Freedom

Nevertheless, freedom is a central theme of the novel, and it is Hannah's attitude toward freedom that Gates and others think identifies her as someone who understands what it means to be a slave. Gates calls this passage, for example, "astonishingly perceptive":

> those who think that the greatest evils of slavery are connected with physical suffering posses [sic] no just or rational ideas of human nature. The soul, the immortal soul must ever long and yearn for a thousand things inseperable [sic] to liberty. Then, too, the fear, the apprehension, the dread, and deep anxiety always attending that condition in a greater or less degree. There can be no certainty, no abiding confidence in any good thing.

Earlier in the novel, there is another passage relating to freedom that also beautifully characterizes Hannah and relates her strong sense of self to Jane's. In one of the novel's gothic scenes, Hannah is sent to close some windows, and to do that, she must walk through a long portrait gallery, wherein hang the portraits of all the former plantation owners and their wives. The sun begins to set, and the shadow of a tree cast on the floor grows "broader and deeper wrapped all in gloom." As Hannah looks at the portrait of her master, it "seems to change from its usually kind and placid expression to one of wrath and gloom," and the brow becomes "wrinkled with passion, the lips turgid with malevolence." This would seem to be the perfect opportunity for Hannah to feel trapped by all the centuries of enslavement that her race has endured, but she instead enters a new world of thoughts, feelings, and sentiments:

> I was not a slave with these pictured memorials of the past. They could not enforce drudgery, or condemn me on account of my color to a life of servitude. As their companion I could think and speculate. In their presence my mind seemed to run riotous and exult in its freedom as a rational being, and one destined for something higher and better than this world can afford.

In the face of the portraits of the dead, Hannah rejoices that in the hereafter, there will be equality and freedom. Here, Hannah has no drum to beat; she sees something of herself in those portraits of her masters and imagines a time and a place of companionability and equality, where "rational beings" might look one another in the eye and stand shoulder to shoulder. This passage is reminiscent of Jane's angry response to Mr. Rochester when she believes he is toying with her affections:

> Do you think, because I am poor, obscure, plain, and little, I am soulless and heartless? You think wrong—I have as much soul as you,—and full as much heart. . . . I am not talking to you now through the medium of custom, conventionalities, nor even of mortal flesh;—it is my spirit that addresses your spirit; just as if both had passed through the grave, and we stood at God's feet, equal,—as we are.

Hannah's powerful spirit also addresses the spirits of her assembled masters.

As the novel progresses, Hannah and her mistress, still on the run, take refuge with some kindly souls in a lovely cottage, only to find that the mistress of the house is Trappe's sister. (The novel is replete with coincidences that strain credibility.) They are recaptured, but the mistress manages to escape to freedom through death. During a conversation with Trappe, a blood vessel bursts and she bleeds to death. As she dies, Hannah tells us, "A gleam of satisfaction shone over her face. There was a gasp, a struggle, a slight shiver of the limbs, and she was free."

The Satiric Edge

In addition to elements of melodrama, gothic gloominess, and sentimentality, *The Bondwoman's Narrative* also contains scenes of sharp, biting satire, many of which are associated with Hannah's second mistress, Mrs. Wheeler. When she first encounters Mrs. Wheeler, Hannah is asked to do her hair. Mrs. Wheeler is both imperious and cranky as poor Hannah struggles to comb out the tangles that have been allowed to accumulate in her hair since her slave, Jane Johnson, ran away the week before. In this very funny scene, Crafts portrays Mrs. Wheeler as virtually incapable of moving or doing anything for herself. Despite pulling at Mrs. Wheeler's tangles, Hannah passes the test, and Mrs. Wheeler determines to buy her from her new master who has never seen her but is on his way to pick her up. She dictates a letter that is to be sent to her prospective master. In it, she characterizes Hannah as "very homely," "a bigot in religion," and "likely to run away at the first opportunity" in order to drive the price down. "No one can doubt that I hesitated to pen such a libel on myself," Hannah notes.

The satire continues when Hannah accompanies Mr. and Mrs. Wheeler to Washington, D. C., where Wheeler tries to get a government appointment after having been relieved of the ambassadorship to Nicaragua. As if to signal to the reader the nature of the satire to come, Crafts opens the chapter with an imitation of the opening paragraphs of Dickens' satirical novel *Bleak House*, in which Dickens begins,

> London. Michaelmas term lately over and the Lord Chancellor sitting in Lincoln's Inn Hall. Implacable November weather. As much mud in the streets as if the waters had but newly retired from the face of the earth, and it would not be wonderful to meet a Megalosaurus, forty feet long or so, waddling like an elephantine lizard up Holborn Hill.

The Washington chapter of *The Bondwoman's Narrative* begins,

> Washington, the Federal City. Christmas holidays recently over. The implacable winter weather. The great President of the Great Republic looks perhaps from the windows of his drawing room . . .

Bleak House continues,

> Fog everywhere. Fog up the river, where it flows among green aits and meadows; fog down the river, where it rolls defiled among the tiers of shipping and the waterside pollutions of a great (and dirty) city."

The Bondwoman's Narrative continues,

> Gloom everywhere. Gloom up the Potomac; where it rolls among the meadows no longer green, and by splendid country seats. Gloom down the Potomac, where it washes the sides of huge warships.

In this chapter, Mrs. Wheeler receives her comeuppance in true Dickensian style. (Dickens' characters most frequently bring their punishments on themselves through their own vanity and foolishness.) When her husband persuades her to use her beauty to help him find a government job, she dusts her face with an expensive power she has sent Hannah to fetch, demands her smelling salts, and sets off. What the reader discovers when she returns from her errand is that the combination of the salts and the powder have turned her face black. It is only on her return that Mrs. Wheeler understands why she was subject to dismissive and insulting behavior during her errand. Whereas the lesson about skin color is lost on Mrs. Wheeler, it is certainly not lost on the reader.

While in Washington, Hannah runs into Lizzy, a fellow slave from Lindendale, the plantation of her birth, who tells her the dreadful story of the new master and his wife. (Hannah's former master hanged himself when he learned that his wife had African blood.) This tale is sexually frank, spectacularly gruesome in detail, and according to some scholars, additional evidence that *The Bondwoman's Narrative* was written by someone who has experienced slavery. The new master of Lindendale has children with several of the most attractive slave women. Because the house is large and rambling and because he can command the staff to complete secrecy, he manages to hide all this from his aristocratic British wife—for a time. When she finds out, she demands he sell the women and their children. After some resistance, he calls the women and their children together and announces they will be sold. Then Crafts tells us,

> **At length one of the youngest and most beautiful, with an infant at her breast hastily dried her tears. Her eyes had a wild phrenzied look, and with a motion so sudden that no one could prevent it, she snatched a sharp knife which a servant had carelessly left after cutting butcher's meat, and stabbing the infant threw it with one toss into the arms of its father. Before he had time to recover from his astonishment she had run the knife into her own body, and fell at his feet bathing them in her blood.**

Lizzy goes on to narrate subsequent events in the lives of the new master and mistress of Lindendale. Clearly, the rest of this sordid tale, which ends with the mistress's death, is Crafts' attempt to demonstrate that the sexual slavery of women, the repeated rape of black women in order to add to the slave population, is as destructive to the masters as it is to the slaves. Their marriage is destroyed, their lives are ruined, and at the end, the house is sold and the portraits that so impressed Hannah are sold on the block, just like so many slaves. Hannah notes on several occasions that she feels liberty is a prerequisite to marriage, and that slaves who are not their own masters are in no position to make sacred vows to one another. She continually implies that to marry and bear children under the system of slavery is immoral, whether rape is involved or not, because it is immoral to condemn infants to a life of servitude.

Escape

This very notion finally convinces Hannah to attempt to escape from slavery. When she and the Wheelers return to the plantation from Washington—to avoid the humiliation that resulted from Mrs. Wheeler's episode in blackface—Mrs. Wheeler accuses Hannah of failing to keep her secret and telling the story around the plantation. Although Hannah denies this vehemently, Mrs. Wheeler does not believe her and tells her she must become a field slave and marry a field slave named Bill. Hannah is horrified and begins to weep, to which Mrs. Wheeler responds, "'With all your pretty airs and your white face, you are nothing but a slave after all, and no better than the blackest wench. Your pride shall be broke, your haughty spirit bought down, and now get you gone.'"

Hannah's horror at this prospect is vivid. She regards herself as "doomed to association with the vile, foul, filthy inhabitants of the huts, and condemned to receive one of them for my husband, my soul actually revolted with horror unspeakable." This is certainly a problematic passage. One might ask Hannah what has happened to her notions of equality and her ideas about the superficiality of skin color as an index of worth. Earlier, however, Hannah makes it clear that she attributes the vile state of the field slaves to the system of slavery itself:

> Degradation, neglect, and ill treatment had wrought on
> them its legitimate effects. All day they toil beneath the
> burning sun, scarcely conscious that any link exists between

themselves and other portions of the human race. Their mental condition is briefly summed up in the phrase that they
know nothing.

Thus, Hannah's horror is directed toward what slavery does to
people. Their state is not a result of any inherent inferiority; anyone
would be degraded by their treatment.

Hannah disguises herself as a boy and leaves the plantation. She meets up with two other fugitive slaves, both of whom
eventually die. She nearly drowns when a boat overturns, but
she is rescued by Aunt Hetty, the woman who taught her how to
read (yet another coincidence). Like most fugitive slaves, Hannah provides little or no detail about her escape route for fear
of alerting those who hunt fugitives. Along the way, she hears
two men talking about the death of Mr. Trappe; he is killed by
the sons of a woman whose life he ruined by exposing her racial
heritage.

The novel has an appropriate ending for a sentimental or
domestic novel. Such works usually end with the heroine happily
married, living in a quaint cottage, and surrounded by friends and
family. Indeed, this is how *The Bondwoman's Narrative* ends. Although Hannah escapes by passing as a white person, when she
arrives in the North, she chooses not to continue to pass but to
live in a black community in New Jersey. She marries a Methodist
minister, a black man who had never been enslaved, and works as
a teacher.

In a final pair of coincidences, Hannah discovers that a
couple she had earlier helped to escape live nearby—as does
her mother, whom she had never seen but who was able to re-
member "certain marks" on Hannah's body and identify her as
her daughter. One scholar regards this ending as conventional
and typical if penned by a white woman but as an extraordinary
exercise in hope and optimism if written by a black woman. Most
of the well-known slave narratives of the period end their tales
on a much more ambiguous note. Freedom is not quite what
the fugitive slaves hoped it would be. Racism and discrimination
are prevalent in the North, and happy endings are not common.
Perhaps the real Hannah truly did find a fairy-tale ending; or,
perhaps she did not but created one out of her fine imagination.
Like Martin Luther King Jr. more than a century later, Hannah
Crafts, too, had a dream.

Slaves' Voices in the Civil War

In 2008, historian Andrew Ward published *The Slaves' War: The Civil War in the Words of Former Slaves*. After years of studying the Civil War, Ward says, he began to want to hear about the events "in the voices of the very people it so imperfectly freed." Thus, he spent years combing through "literally thousands of interviews, obituaries, squibs, diaries, letters, memoirs, and depositions" taken from or left by former slaves. Ward has assembled "an account of the war as it was remembered and construed and imagined by enslaved civilians: a retrospective view from the fields, the kitchens, the slave quarters, the roadsides, the swamps, the camps, the battlefields—a back-door, ground-level slant on the savagery that changed their posterity; and their country forever."

Many of these voices speak in what Ward calls "a luminous vernacular," a kind of folk POETIC DICTION that gives their statements and observations a universal appeal.

Yankees and Abe Lincoln

Despite their boasting that the Yankees would not last six weeks in a battle with southern manhood, white plantation owners were afraid that their slaves would run away or betray the southern cause. Oblivious to the grapevine that kept slaves fairly well informed about what was going on, slave owners made every effort to portray Yankees as demons. Many slaves believed their masters at first, and their descriptions of Yankees had a fairy-tale quality. One slave was afraid that "the Yankees gonna get us and cut our necks off." Alice Johnson of Arkansas said, "I used to hear them talking about the Yankees, and I didn't know if they was horses or mules or varmints or folks or what not."

However, it did not take long for the slaves to see through the propaganda. One individual quoted by Ward noted that, as the war dragged on, "the white folks didn't try to scare us about the Yankees cause they was too scared theirselves." Another was fine once a Yankee solder took off his hat to prove he did not have horns. Another said after his first encounter with a Yankee, "Why, they's folks!"

Southerners also attempted to demonize President Abraham Lincoln (1861–1865). Nevertheless, many slaves reimagined Lincoln as a mythical figure whom Ward describes as a sort of "furtive abolitionist phantom swirling through Dixie, stirring up slaves

Contrabands Coming Into Camp
During the Civil War (1861–1865), many slaves escaped from their masters and fled to Union camps. At first, the Union declared the slaves "contraband," property that now belonged to the union as a result of the state of war between the North and South. These individuals were initially put to work without compensation, but in 1861, Secretary of the Navy Gideon Wells issued an order requiring that "persons of color commonly known as contrabands" be paid. The Army quickly issued a similar order.

▪ ▪ ▪ ▪ CONTRABAND ▪ ▪ ▪ ▪

Contraband is defined as "goods or merchandise whose importation, exportation, or possession is forbidden . . . smuggled goods." The term *contraband* was also used to describe African American slaves who had escaped or had been captured behind Union lines during the Civil War. The term was coined in 1861 by Union General Benjamin Butler, and its use is sadly IRONIC. As slaves began to flee plantations and seek refuge behind Union lines, some Union commanders, believing that the law required them to return "property," actually sent captives back to their masters. Butler, a lawyer, got around the issue by declaring escaped slaves to be contraband, the spoils of war, which could legally be seized by the army.

Butler commanded the Union Fort Monroe in Hampton Roads, Virginia. After his decision about how to treat fugitive slaves, thousands flocked to the fort—so many, in fact, they could no longer stay inside the walls. The contrabands began to settle in the ruined city of Hampton. They built houses and even named their settlement Grand Contraband Camp. By the end of the war, more than ten thousand people lived in and around Grand Contraband Camp.

and masters." In some stories, Lincoln becomes a LITMUS TEST for kindness and hospitality. Treated well, he warns families of the war to come; treated badly, he becomes an avenger. At one home where he feasted on "chicken hash and batter cakes and dried venison," he tells the master, "If you free the people, I'll bring you back into the Union." If the master refuses, however, Lincoln tells him, "I'll whip you back into the Union." In the minds of slaves, Lincoln was a great man with great powers, but he thought, talked, and felt as they did. One woman said her mother told her that Lincoln traveled the South as a beggar "and found out everything." He returned to the North and explained "how slavery was ruining the nation."

During the war, slaves were continually made aware of their masters' hatred of Lincoln. George Womble reported that his master planned to use Lincoln's skull "as a soap dish." Slaves were severely punished for any demonstration of admiration for Lincoln. Mattie Jackson recounts an incident involving her mother,

Another contraband camp near Corinth, Mississippi, served as a model for other camps. By 1863, it was home to nearly four thousand former slaves who built their own houses, grew food in kitchen gardens, and helped the Union Army with their labor. However, in many other camps, residents suffered from lack of food and shelter, and many died of various diseases.

In 1863, a photographer and artist, Alfred Waud, published a sketch in *Harper's Weekly* entitled "Contrabands Coming into Camp." He commented on the drawing, as well:

> *There is something very touching in seeing these poor people coming into camp— giving up all the little ties that cluster about home, such as it is in slavery, and trustfully throwing themselves on the mercy of the Yankees, in the hope of getting permission to own themselves and keep their children from the auction block. This party [in the drawing] evidently comprises a whole family. . . .*

Many of the contraband camps that sprang up during the war became the first African American neighborhoods in the south and the basis for African American urban neighborhoods in general.

whose master found a newspaper clipping with Lincoln's picture among her things, "He knocked her down three times, and sent her to the trader's yard [where slaves were bought and sold] for a month as punishment."

Thus, in 1865, it should come as no surprise that many slaves were devastated by Lincoln's assassination. Ward reports that the Secretary of the Navy, Gideon Wells, saw hundreds of recently freed slaves gathered near the White House. He said he was deeply affected by the crowd's "hopeless grief." Jackson walked past Lincoln's coffin. "The death of the President was like an electric shock to my soul," she wrote. "I could not feel convinced of his death until I gazed upon his remains, and heard the last roll of the muffled drum and the farewell boom of the cannon. I was then convinced that though we were left to the tender mercies of God, we were without a leader." According to Ward, "In their grief and shock, black people believed, with some justification, that Lincoln's assassination was part of a conspiracy against them."

Ward notes that not every slave admired Lincoln; some felt that he got too much credit for what was, in fact, God's will. Others felt that freedom without a way to make a living was not much of a blessing. Many felt that freeing the slaves was not nearly as important to Lincoln as preserving the union. Still, most of Ward's informants tended to regard Lincoln as almost a "biblical" figure, "next to God," some thought, and "greater than Moses." According to Charles Willis, Lincoln "done more for us than any man done since Jesus left."

The Aftermath of War

One scene was repeated again and again throughout the South when the war ended. Slaveholders, sometimes with a Union soldier standing by as a witness, called the slaves together to tell them that they were free. One slave remembers her master saying, "You-all don't belong to me no more. You and Wesley and the childrens: you just belong to yourselfs." Another slave remembered his master saying, "Now you is all free! Just as free as I am. Don't belong to me, or no one: onliest yourselves." This same slave remembers that no one reacted at first, "only stand there." It must have taken some time for the concept of freedom to sink in.

Some masters delayed the news as long as they could—in some cases they said nothing for months. Beatrice Black said, "I reckon they was right smart old masers what didn't want to let they slaves go after freedom. They hated to turn them loose. Just let them work on. Heap of them didn't know freedom come. I used to hear tell how the government had to send soldiers away down in the far backcountry to make them turn the slaves loose. Other masters continued to mete out punishments as if they still owned the slaves. Another slave woman, upon hearing she was free, began to shout "Thank God-a-Mighty." Her master "come and knocked her down." She "fainted dead away then, because she wanted to holler so bad and was scared to make a sound." Yet another former slave remembered that when people began to shout "Thank the Lawd, us is free as the jay birds," a white stranger threatened to kill them if he ever heard anyone say such a thing again.

Ward notes that "some of the most exuberant celebrations" occurred among slaves who found out they were free while working in the fields. One woman "dropped her hoe and danced out to the turn road and dance right up into Old Master's parlor. She went so fast a bird could not have held on to her dress tail. That night she sent and got all the neighbors, and they danced all night long." Other masters and slaves cried. Andrew Jackson Gill remembered that his mistress "stood there tall and straight, and tried to smile. But I see'd a tear a-trickling off her nose, and pretty soon we was all crying together."

Freedom proved to be an elusive promise for many former slaves, and many celebrations were short lived as people began to realize that they owned less than nothing—some owners threatened to rip the clothes off their backs—and had nowhere to go. John McAdams said he "expected different from what I got out of freedom, I can tell you. I knows one thing: I was not expecting to be turned loose like a bunch of stray cattle." Another former slave lamented that "all the folks soon scatter all over. But if they all like me, they still have to work just as hard, and sometimes have less than we used to have." Freedom was a bittersweet prize.

Literary Voices

Two other writers bear mentioning in this chapter—Frances E. W. Harper (1825–1911) and Paul Laurence Dunbar (1872–1906). Harper published the first short story by an African American and is also known as the first African American journalist, and Dunbar was the first African American poet to be widely read by both blacks and whites. While Harper's and Dunbar's voices were not "unmediated," like that of Hannah Crafts or the speakers in historian Andrew Ward's work, both were clearly talented and influential. Dunbar, in particular, influenced the writers of the early twentieth-century literary and social phenomenon known as the Harlem Renaissance. While Crafts' work has more historical than literary value, Dunbar and Harper are certainly remembered for their literary contributions.

Harper had a long career. She published her first poems at the age of 20 and her novel *Iola Leroy* (1892) at the age of 67. In *Iola Leroy*, Harper—who herself was born free—depicts a slave family's efforts to reunite after emancipation. Unfortunately, her first volume of poetry, *Forest Leaves* (1845) has been lost. Her second volume, *Poems of Miscellaneous Subjects* (1854) was extremely popular among both blacks and whites, so much so that it was reprinted 20 times. One of her best-loved poems, "Bury Me in a Free Land," was published just before the end of the Civil War. The form of the poem is conventional, written in stanzas of four tetrameter lines, rhyming aabb. Despite the constraints imposed by the form, the poem makes a powerful statement using violent imagery. The speaker begins by saying that she is not concerned about where she is buried, as long as it is not in "a land where men are slaves." She says she could not rest if surrounded by the awful accompaniments of slavery: the sound of the lash, the shrieks of mothers whose children are torn from their arms, the "bay/Of bloodhounds seizing their human prey," the captive who pleads in vain "as they bound afresh his galling chain." The poem ends:

> I ask no monument, proud and high
> To arrest the gaze of the passers-by;
> All that my yearning spirit craves,
> Is bury me not in a land of slaves.

Ironically, as popular as her work was in her lifetime, Harper was not a favorite of literary critics. Even W.E. B. Dubois (1868–1963) denigrated her work: "She was not a great singer, but she had some sense of song; she was not a great writer, but she wrote much worth reading." Eventually her gravestone toppled and was covered with grass. Recently, however, African American and feminist critics have urged readers to take another look at Harper's work. On the hundredth anniversary of the publication of *Iola Leroy*, African American Unitarian Universalists honored Harper by installing a new gravestone.

In contrast to Harper, Dunbar had an extraordinarily short life. He died of tuberculosis at the age of 33. Like Harper, Dunbar's poetry was popular with both black and white audiences. Dunbar, however, was also touted by the literary establishment. No less a critic than William Dean Howells wrote the introduction to Dunbar's second volume of published poetry, *Majors and Minors* (1895). To Dunbar's chagrin, however, Howells particularly liked Dunbar's dialect poetry. Of the dialect verse, Holmes said:

> Paul Dunbar was the only man of pure African blood and of American civilization to feel the negro life aesthetically and express it lyrically. It seemed to me that this had come to its most modern consciousness in him, and that his brilliant and

unique achievement was to have studied the American negro objectively, and to have represented him as he found him to be, with humor, with sympathy, and yet with what the reader must instinctively feel to be entire truthfulness.

Dunbar himself preferred his poems written in standard English and felt circumscribed by his audience's preferences and expectations. One of his best-known poems expresses his sense of being trapped in a stereotype. It was from this poem that the contemporary writer Maya Angelou took the title of her famous autobiography, *I Know Why the Caged Bird Sings*. The Dunbar poem, entitled "Sympathy," begins "I know what the caged bird feels, alas!/When the sun is bright on the upland slopes." He goes on to say that the bird "beats his wing/Till its blood is red on the cruel bars," because he must stay on his perch when he'd rather fly free. The poet adds that the caged bird sings "not a carol of joy or glee/But a prayer that he sends from his heart's deep core," a prayer for freedom both to be and do what one pleases.

While Dunbar may not have liked his dialect poetry as much as some of his other works, he, like the great American storyteller Mark Twain, was able to use dialect to express the dignity and pride of African Americans. In his well-known "When Malindy Sings," for example, the speaker calls to "Miss Lucy," no doubt the white mistress, to "quit dat noise," as Lucy tried to sing. She cannot, he says, hold a candle to Malindy. The final verse makes it clear that Malindy's song exists in memory only but is breathtakingly beautiful:

> Towsah, stop dat ba'kin', hyeah me!
>   Mandy, mek dat chile keep still;
> Don't you hyeah de echoes callin'
>   F'om de valley to de hill?
> Let me listen, I can hyeah it,
>   Th'oo de bresh of angels' wings,
> Sof' an' sweet, "Swing Low, Sweet Chariot,"
>   Ez Malindy sings.

Despite his brief life, Dunbar was extraordinarily prolific, writing not only 12 volumes of poetry, four collections of short stories, a play, and five novels but also the lyrics for *In Dahomey*, the first musical comedy performed by a completely African American cast to appear on Broadway.

For too long, the voices of African Americans remained unheard in America. In the years just before and just after the Civil War, what was a murmer became a chorus. African Americans were heard across the land; their nineteenth-century voices helped establish a distinctly American literature.

T i m e l i n e

Science, Technology, and the Arts	Literature	History
1852 Elisha Otis invents a brake for passenger elevators **1854** **1855**	Hawthorne *The Blithdale Romance* Stowe *Uncle Tom's Cabin* Thoreau *Walden* Whitman *Leaves of Grass* (1st ed.)	Franklin Pierce elected president
1857 **1859**	Hannah Crafts completes *The Bondwoman's Narrative* Wilson *Our Nig* Melville *The Confidence Man*	Mexico prohibits slavery
1860 Pony Express begins	Emily Dickinson writing poems	Abraham Lincoln elected Start of Civil War 10 states secede from Union
1861	Jacobs *Incidents in the Life of a Slave Girl*	Lincoln re-elected
1862		Morrill Land Grant Colleges Act General Robert E. Lee placed in command of Confederate forces
1863 **1864** Pullman constructs the sleeping car for railroads	Lincoln *Gettysburg Address* Death of Nathaniel Hawthorne Carroll *Alice's Adventures in Wonderland*	New York Draft Riots Grant placed in charge of all Union forces
1865 Wagner *Tristan und Isolde* **1866** Homer *The Morning Bell* **1867** Alfred Nobel patents dynamite	Twain "The Celebrated Jumping Frog of Calaveras County" Whittier "Snowbound"	Lincoln assassinated Civil War ends 14th Amendment granting freedom to all blacks as full citizens
1868	Alcott *Little Women*	Eight-hour day for Federal employees Grant elected president
1869 Westinghouse invents the air brake **1869** Union Pacific and Central Pacific railroads meet **1869** Suez Canal opens **1870** Britain makes education compulsory	Alger *Ragged Dick* Twain *The Innocents Abroad* Harte *The Luck of Roaring Camp*	Population for NY: 1,478,103 Chicago 298,977 Boston 250,526 Denver 4749 Los Angeles 5728

Science, Technology, and the Arts	Literature	History
1871 James Whistler *Whistler's Mother*	William Dean Howells becomes editor of *The Atlantic Monthly* Eggleston *The Hoosier Schoolmaster*	
1872 Elijah McCoy invents the automatic engine oiler	Eliot *Middlemarch* Twain *Roughing It* Twain and Warner *The Gilded Age*	Grant reelected Yellowstone National Park created
1873 **1874** Stephen Dudley Field produces an electric streetcar **1874** First Impressionist art exhibit in Paris		
1876 Alexander Graham Bell invents the telephone	Twain *The Adventures of Tom Sawyer* Carroll *The Hunting of the Snark* James *The American*	American centennial
1877 Thomas Alva Edison invents the phonograph **1878** Anna Baldwin develops the first milking machine **1879** Edison makes the first incandescent light bulb	Cable *Old Creole Days* James *Daisy Miller* Cable *The Grandissimes* Adams *Democracy, An American Novel* James *The Portrait of a Lady*	
1880		
1881 Booker T. Washington establishes Tuskeegee Institute **1882** Standard Oil conglomerate controls the oil industry Liszt *Hungarian Rhapsody* Wagner *Parsifal* Manet *A Bar at the Folies Bergere* **1883** Shoemaking machine invented by Jan Matzeliger **1884** Lewis Waterman makes the first fountain pen **1885** Pasteur administers successful rabies vaccine	Douglass *The Life and Times of Frederick Douglass* Howells *A Modern Instance* Twain *The Prince and the Pauper* Howells *A Modern Instance* Twain *Life on the Mississippi* Jewett *A Country Doctor* Howells *The Rise of Silas Lapham* Twain *Adventures of Huckleberry Finn*	James Garfield inaugurated James Garfield assassinated

Science, Technology, and the Arts	Literature	History
1886 Japan uses electricity Statue of Liberty dedicated (gift from France)	Edward Bellamy *Looking Backward* James *The Princess Cassimassima* Death of Emily Dickinson	Haymarket Riots American Federation of Labor (AFL) formed
1887 Automatic air brake invented by Granville T. Woods		
1888 Amateur photography begins with Eastman Kodak's camera	Death of Edward Lear	National Geographic Society founded Sherman antitrust act tries to ensure business competition Famous blizzard of '88 in New York City
1889 First U.S. Film *Fred Ott's Sneeze*	Twain *A Connecticut Yankee in King Arthur's Court* Yeats *The Wanderings of Oisin*	
1890 Van Gogh paints his greatest pictures, commits suicide	Howells *A Hazard of New Fortunes*	Yosemite National Park founded Massacre at Wounded Knee Wyoming admitted to the US
1891	Death of Herman Melville Bierce *Tales of Soldiers and Civilians* Garland *Main-Travelled Roads*	US international copyright bill
1892	Gilman *The Yellow Wallpaper* McClure's Magazine founded	Columbian exposition New Zealand permits women to vote
1893 The Duryea brothers make the first gasoline powered car	Crane *Maggie a Girl of the Streets*	
1894	Chopin *Bayou Folk*	Federal Court rules Pullman strike against the law
1895 Wilhelm Roentgen discovers X-rays **1895** King Gillette makes a safety razor with disposable blades	Twain *Pudd'nhead Wilson* Crane *The Red Badge of Courage* Death of Frederick Douglass Jewett *Country of the Pointed Firs* James *What Maisie Knew*	

Science, Technology, and the Arts	Literature	History
1896	James *The Spoils of Poynton*	William McKinley elected president Annexation of Hawaii *Plessy v. Ferguson* affirms idea of "separate but equal" Klondike gold rush
1897 **1898** M. et Mme. Curie discover radium **1899** The motor driven vacuum cleaner made by John Thurman Scott Joplin *The Maple Leaf Rag* **1900** Planck's quantum theory Freud publishes *The Interpretation of Dreams*	Finley Peter Dunne *Mr. Dooley in Peace and War* James *The Turn of the Screw* Chopin *The Awakening* Norris *McTeague* Dreiser *Sister Carrie* Conrad *Lord Jim*	Spanish-American war Population for NY: 3,437,202 Chicago 1,698,575 Boston 560,892 Denver 133,859 Los Angeles 102,479
1901 First transatlantic wireless message sent **1902** Macys opens a 9-story department store Scott Joplin *The Entertainer* **1903**	Norris *The Octopus* James *The Wings of the Dove* DuBois *The Souls of Black Folk* James *The Ambassadors* London *The Call of the Wild* Norris *The Octopus*	McKinley shot; Roosevelt president Death of Queen Victoria End of the Boer War Wright brothers fly airplane in NC
1904 New York subway system opened **1905** Einstein, Theory of Relativity	James *The Golden Bowl* London *The Sea-Wolf* Wharton *The House of Mirth* Chesnutt *The Colonel's Dream*	
1906 **1907** Steiglitz *The Steerage* **1908** General Electric patents electric toaster **1909** Leo Baekeland makes plastic French aviator flies across the English Channel	London *White Fang* Sinclair *The Jungle* London *Martin Eden* T. S. Eliot "The Love Song of J. Alfred Prufrock"	Pure Food and Drug Act

Science, Technology, and the Arts	Literature	History
1910 Rousseau *The Dream* **1911** **1913** Henry Ford uses assembly line to make automobiles **1914** **1915** **1916** **1920** **1925**	Death of Mark Twain Wharton *Ethan Frome* Dreiser *Jennie Gerhardt* Wharton *The Custom of the Country* Dreiser *The Financier* Booker T. Washington dies Death of Henry James and Jack London Wharton *The Age of Innocence* Dreiser *An American Tragedy*	Federal Reserve Act passed regulating the banking industry World War I begins The Jazz Age begins

Glossary of Terms

abolitionist a person who advocated ending slavery

aestheticism the belief that the aim of art and life is to produce beauty

allusion the act of indirectly referring to something, often to historical events, works of literature, or ideas and concepts

archetypical perfectly representative of a class

authenticate to verify the authenticity of an object or document

balance a rhetorical device—the use of phrases of approximately equal length

Bowdlerize to sanitize a piece of writing by cutting out or changing supposedly offensive language or situations. Derived from Thomas Bowdler, an English physician who in 1818 published such an edition of Shakespeare

burlesque a ludicrous exaggeration

catholic universal, when spelled with lower-case "c"

census an official count or numbering of a country's population

cliché a trite, often heard phrase or idea

color line the boundary marking one race from another, usually thought of in terms of percentage of blood line

comedy of manners a novel or play that satirizes social customs and distinctions

communal referring to or having to do with a community

communism the dictatorship of the ordinary people for the sake of the ordinary people. Socialism does not advocate such a dictatorship. Vladimir Lenin thought socialism the first step toward Communism

costume drama a play or novel in which the characters lack depth and are identified by their clothes

determinism the belief that every action or thought has been shaped by forces outside the will

didactic intending to teach or inculcate a lesson, usually a moral one

domestic literature works that focus on the interests and lives of women readers; the plots of such works are similar, involving young girls who have to make their way in the world and who succeed in marrying well; works that are based on a notion of the goodness of human nature and the idea that feelings can guide people to make good choices; also called sentimental literature

elegaic adjective describing a poem or other utterance expressing sorrow

emendation the act or practice of altering or correcting

epigraph a brief quotation at the beginning of a literary work that suggests its theme

epitaph an inscription on a tombstone

exposé a true but unflattering portrait of a person or condition, from the French for *exposed*

fiasco a complete failure

formulaic following an established pattern

Free Labor the key plank of the political platform of the Free Soil Party, formed in 1848 to advance the cause of "free soil, free speech, free labor, and free men." In 1854 the Free Soilers disbanded and their cause was embraced by the newly formed Republican party

genteel refined; relating to the gentry or upper class

historiography the writing of history

icon originally a symbolic religious figure worshipped as a saint, now come to mean a symbol of a set of beliefs or practices

ingénue a young woman who is innocent of the ways of the world

ironic characterized by a difference or incongruity between what is expected and what is

limited omniscient point of view a perspective in which the writer concentrates on what one character can know, although the story is told from the third person

literature of witness a novel or account written by one who actually saw the events

literary realism a series of conventions designed to make a literary work seem to be a faithful representation of reality

litmus test literally a test for chemical activity using litmus paper; figuratively, a test that uses a single indicator to make a decision

local color writing writing that uses the speech and habits of a region to create atmosphere

malign to make evil or harmful statements about someone or something

metaphor a comparison, in which one idea or object is identified with another: e. g., "farming was life itself to the Midwesterner"

milieux literally *locations*; referring to physical or social settings in which events occur

muckraker one who digs up dirt for the purpose of exposing corruption and injustice

naturalism a literary movement emphasizing the role of environment and heredity on human life and action

nostalgic a yearning for the past, when times were better

novella a short novel

omniscient narrator in literature, a point of view through which a story is told. An omniscient narrator is all-seeing and all-knowing and can "travel" from one location in the novel to another, looking into the hearts and minds of all the characters

parable a fable that points to a lesson by creating characters of symbolic import

parallelism the repeated use of similar grammatical structures for rhetorical effect

paean a song of praise

picaresque a form of novel in which a series of adventures occur in a series to one figure, usually a villain or rogue

poetaster a would-be or inferior poet

poetic diction the style of language and choice of words often used in poetry; William Wordsworth and other Romantic poets advocated the use of more conversational language in poetry

point of view the perspective from which a narrative or essay comes. Fiction is usually told from the first person point of view ("I" or "we"), the third person ("omniscient" or "all knowing") or limited third person (in which authors restrict themselves to what is known by only one person)

propagandist one who is more interested in espousing a cause than in entertaining or analyzing

progressives people who see themselves as advocates of positive social reform

protest writers authors who object strenuously to social, economic, political ills

pseudonym pen name; many writers in the past wrote under other names, for a variety of reasons

psychological realism a form of realism that focuses on the workings of the mind or perception

realist a writer who believes that it is more important to adhere to concrete facts than to present idealized versions of existence

regionalists writers associated with one area or locale

rhetorical balance the setting forth of similar grammatical elements of approximately the same length for a formal, pleasing symmetry

satirist one who uses humor to criticize and expose foolishness or evil

sentimental indulging in emotion for the sake of that emotion—a negative term

sentimental literature works that focus on the interests and lives of women readers; the plots of such works are similar, involving young girls who have to make their way in the world and who succeed in marrying well; works that are based on a notion of the goodness of human nature and the idea that feelings can guide people to make good choices; also called domestic literature

slave narratives stories written by slaves that expose the conditions of their lives

Social Darwinism the idea that in society the strong and able dominate the weak

socialism a system of governance in which all the workers own all the property and work for the common good

subservient submissive; like a servant

tall tale a story so fantastic that it abandons any pretense to actuality and is usually meant to be enjoyed for humorous exaggeration

transcendent that which is beyond the real or the material; going beyond the usual limits

trust a group of corporations that join together to limit competition; now prohibited by U.S. law

übermensch or "superman," the man whose superior intelligence and strength makes him the natural ruler of others

underground railroad the series of safe houses and hiding places slaves used to journey to the North and gain freedom

vade mecum Latin words meaning, literally, "go with me," hence a guidebook or a reference book

vernacular every day speech forms characterized by the use of slang and other racy expressions

verisimilitude having the quality of seeming realistic

Western humor mode of popular writing that features the comic opposition of cultural types, high-brow and low-brow. Especially notable for its representation of the fantastic or grotesque as if they were sober reality

yokel an uneducated, backward inhabitant of any particular region

Biographical Glossary

Alger, Horatio (1832–1899) Horatio Alger started out to be a preacher. His father was a Unitarian minister and closely monitored his son, who graduated from Harvard Divinity School in 1860. The young Alger did not remain in the ministry, leaving it under forced circumstances in 1866. A bachelor, he moved to New York City, where he started writing fiction for boys. In 1868 his first novels appeared, and before his death in 1899 he wrote, or directed the writing of more than 100 similar stories, each of about 50,000 words. His rags to riches formulaic stories, such as *Ragged Dick, Frank Fowler, the Cash Boy,* and others, popularized a basic American myth.

Brontë, Charlotte (1816–1855) English novelist and creator of the famous heroine Jane Eyre. Brontë was born in Yorkshire, England in 1816, the third child of Patrick Brontë, a clergyman, and his wife Maria. In 1821, the family moved to Haworth, where Patrick had been appointed curate. Within a few short months, Maria died of cancer, leaving Patrick with six children to rear. In 1824, Charlotte and her sisters Emily, Maria, and Elizabeth, were sent to boarding school, where the conditions were so poor that Maria and Elizabeth both died of tuberculosis soon after they returned home in 1825. In her novel *Jane Eyre*, Charlotte would portray this school as the infamous Lowood. Upon her return to the parsonage at Haworth, Charlotte and her brother Branwell and sisters Emily and Anne began writing stories and poetry about imaginary kingdoms they called Angria and Gondol. Between 1831 and 1844, Charlotte taught and worked for several families as a governess. In 1846 she and her sisters published an unsuccessful volume of poetry under the names Currer, Ellis, and Acton Bell. The next year Charlotte published her masterpiece, *Jane Eyre*, to great critical acclaim. In 1848, Emily and Branwell died, as did Anne a year later. Charlotte married in 1855 and became pregnant. She and her unborn child died in 1855.

Cather, Willa (1873–1947) The great chronicler of the Midwest was actually born in Virginia but moved to Nebraska when she was four years old. By eleven she was in Red Cloud, the town with which she is most closely associated. After publishing a book of poems and a book of short stories, *The Troll Garden* (1905), which includes the well-known "Paul's Case," she moved to New York City to work for *McClure's Magazine*. An acquaintance with Sarah Orne Jewett gave her a sense of self-confidence, and after one indifferent novel and a return visit to Red Cloud, she wrote the novels that initially made her reputation, *O Pioneers!* (1913), *The Song of the Lark* (1915), and in 1918 *My Ántonia.* Dissatisfied with the inelegant look of her books, she changed publishers with *One of Ours* (1922) and then wrote the novels of nostalgia and a more humane existence that earned her a steady following: *A Lost Lady* (1923), *The Professor's House* (1925), and *Death Comes for the Archbishop* (1927). Her increasing impatience with the modern world and her illnesses forced her to stop writing after 1940, though she continued to receive honors until her death in 1947.

Chesnutt, Mary (1823–1886) Mary Chesnutt wrote three novels—published only after her death. Her importance comes from diaries in which her personal sorrows and those of the world around her are set against the backdrop of the South both before and after the Civil War. Chesnutt writes with all the skill of a professional novelist. She was a witty, ironic, rueful memoirist of subtle candor. She edited her diary, thinking that it would be published, but publication happened only after her death, and it was not published in scholarly form until 1981. As a way of capturing the feel of the times, this is probably the most authentic document of the Civil War.

Chopin, Kate (1850–1904) Born Katherine O'Flahertie in St. Louis, Missouri, Chopin did not move to Louisiana, the state with which her fiction and life are most intimately associated, until her marriage to Oscar Chopin in 1870. Her first novel, *At Fault* (1890), she published herself, but it is her Louisiana stories that resulted in her first commercially published book, *Bayou Folk* (1894). She wrote a second collection of her own work, *A Night in Acadie* (1897) that was not as well received as her previous. The work for which she is best known today, *The Awakening* (1899), caused outrage because of its sexual frankness and seeming amorality. Her health began to fail in her early fifties and she died of a cerebral hemorrhage at 54.

Clemens, Samuel Langhorne, A. K. A. Mark Twain (1835–1910) Although born in Florida, Mark Twain is associated with the Mississippi River. After his steamboating experiences Twain journeyed westward to California, where he started his career as a writer by producing narratives and tales in the tradition of southwestern humor. After establishing himself in Hartford,

Connecticut, where he built an elaborate house that still stands to this day, he wrote the books that made him a world-famous literary figure, *The Adventures of Tom Sawyer* (1875), *The Prince and the Pauper* (1882), *Life on the Mississippi* (1883), and *The Adventures of Huckleberry Finn* (1885). His final years were saddened by the death of his wife and his beloved daughter Susy, the illness of Jean, and increasing loneliness and bitterness, notwithstanding that he lived on Fifth Avenue in New York and enjoyed being a public figure, recognized all over, wearing his white suit. He received an honorary degree from Oxford University in 1907 and died of angina in 1910.

Crane, Stephen (1871–1900) Crane spent his early years in New Jersey where his destitute family moved from town to town. A brief period in a boarding school was followed by brief stays at Lafayette College and Syracuse University. Eventually, he worked as a news writer and, while doing so, wrote his first novel (self-published) *Maggie, a Girl of the Streets.* The book was read by William Dean Howells, who liked it and encouraged Crane. After reading much Civil War literature, Crane wrote and found a publisher for *The Red Badge of Courage* (1896), which made him famous. After working, like Willa Cather, for McClure's syndicate, Crane met Cora Howorth Steward and eventually moved with her to England. In 1897, after various news assignments, he wrote "The Open Boat," "The Bride Comes to Yellow Sky," and, in 1898, "The Blue Hotel." Crane made friends with many famous writers, notably Joseph Conrad and the American Harold Frederic, in England. He developed tuberculosis and died in a German sanitarium at the age of 29.

Douglass, Frederick (1817–1895) After undergoing the events described in his *Narrative,* Douglass became a lecturer, speaking in America, England, and Scotland, before moving to Rochester, New York. He continued writing the story of his life even as he was living it. He wrote "Men of Color to Arms!" After the Civil War, he continued writing and published a magazine of his own. He composed numerous pamphlets. After his wife died, he married a white woman, enraging many who found interracial marriage unacceptable. Despite his prominence, he was not always included in governmental and social functions where he belonged (for example, President Grant did not invite him to the White House). He served as an international ambassador to Haiti. Toward the end of his life, he published *The Life and Times of Frederick Douglass,* revealing details of the Underground Railroad not included in earlier printings. He died of heart failure in 1895.

Dreiser, Theodore (1871–1945) Dirt poor, Dreiser spent his earliest years in Terre Haute, Indiana. His dozen siblings were colorful characters, one of whom, Paul, was a successful songwriter. Early on, Theodore Dreiser's preoccupations, which remained with him his entire life, were women and literature. Working at a variety of jobs—as a driver with a laundry, a real estate salesman, a stock boy at a hardware firm—he eventually landed a job on the St. Louis *Globe-Democrat.* At the urging of a friend, he wrote *Sister Carrie,* which was finally published in 1900, with great reluctance, by Doubleday, Page and Company. Frank Norris supported the book. Editorship of a pulp magazine followed, while Dreiser struggled with his next novel, *Jennie Gerhardt* (1911). In the next few years he published memoirs and novels, including *The Financier* (1912), *The Titan* (1914), and *The Genius* (1915). Following a series of plays and short story collections, he composed his greatest work, *An American Tragedy,* with his steadiest publisher, Liveright, in 1925. He was increasingly drawn to socialism and visited Russia. He married Helen Richardson just a year before his death in 1945.

Grant, Ulysses S. (1822–1885) The general who eventually won the Civil War for the North was an Ohio boy who graduated from the military academy at West Point. Grant had a series of victories in the Civil War, notably at Vicksburg, Mississippi, where he surprised the Confederate army by attacking from the rear. Grant waged total war—depriving civilians as well as armed forces of food and shelter—in his quest for victory. Lee surrendered to Grant in Appamatox, Virginia, in 1865. Later, as the 18th president, Grant was less shrewd than he had been as a general, appointing greedy friends to important government positions. Although he won a second term, Grant's reputation was tarnished. He proved, however, a superb memoirist. His account of the Civil War, published by a publishing company owned by Mark Twain (who thought Grant a better writer than he himself) partly dictated while Grant was dying of throat cancer, was a best seller and remains a central document of its era.

Howells, William Dean (1837–1920) A self-educated man, Howells spent his early years in Ohio writing and publishing locally but moved east in 1859 to pursue a literary career. As editor at *The Atlantic Monthly,* he became friends with Mark Twain and Henry James. Interested in European realism, as well as current social theory, he published several novels on his own and became a full-time writer after resigning his post at *The Atlantic. A Modern Instance* (1882) and his best known work, *The Rise of Silas Lapham* (1885), followed. Subject to depression and worried about his ill daughter Winifred (who died in 1889), Howells began to write in a deeper, more radical tone, especially notable in *A Hazard of New Fortunes* (1890). He was, by this time, America's prime example of a man of letters. However, he found himself increasingly out of touch with American writing and culture; his audience had gone. He died in 1920 of pneumonia.

James, Henry (1843–1916) Born into a well-known and accomplished family (his brother William was the distinguished American pragmatist philosopher), James spent his early years in New York and eventually entered Harvard Law School, from which he withdrew in order to devote his time to writing. After some years in Boston, where he made the acquaintance of William Dean Howells, James sailed for Europe in 1870. Increasingly Europe drew him, and after publishing *The American* in 1877, he centered his literary and social life in England. He became something of a social lion, writing in 1879 that he had "dined out the past winter 107 times!" *Daisy Miller* (1878), his one popular success, was followed by *The Portrait of a Lady* (1882) and *The Princess Cassimassima* (1886). Continuing an impressive spate of fictive, critical, and travel writings, James tried to branch into a career as a playwright with *Guy Domville* (1895), but the play was poorly received and James returned to fiction with *The Spoils of Poynton* (1897) and the three novels in his grand, final manner, which he dictated: *The Wings of the Dove* (1902), *The Ambassadors* (1903), and *The Golden Bowl* (1904), all while writing short stories and criticism, and socializing. In 1915, after working with wounded soldiers, he decided to become a British citizen. After a stroke, he developed pneumonia and died early in 1916.

Jacobs, Harriet (1813–1897) Jacobs was born in Edenton, North Carolina, where she was sent to live in the household of a physician, Dr. James Norcom, who made sexual overtures to her. After forming a secret relationship with a lawyer in Edenton by whom she had two children, she went into hiding in hopes that Norcom would sell her children to her lover, as in fact happened. She escaped by a slave ship to Philadelphia and found work in New York. To avoid capture, she moved to Boston and then to Rochester, New York, where the wife of one of her former protectors purchased her freedom in 1852. Her manuscript,

Incidents in the Life of a Slave Girl (1861) was published anonymously in 1861. Jacobs died in Washington in 1897.

Jewett, Sarah Orne (1849–1909) Born in South Berwick, Maine, Jewett at first intended to pursue a career in medicine and at the same time published stories about her native state. William Dean Howells encouraged her to expand some of these into a full-length novel, later called *Deephaven,* which was published to good reviews. Her second novel *A Country Doctor* (1884), with its female protagonist, was based partly on her own early interests. The four parts of her best-known book, *The Country of the Pointed Firs* (1896), were published in *The Atlantic Monthly* before appearing as a book. With Fields, she traveled widely. Acquainted with all the major literary figures of her day, Jewett was plagued throughout her life by rheumatism and ill health. Before her death at sixty she produced one popular novel, *The Tory Lover,* not set in Maine and more patently an escape than her best work.

Lincoln, Abraham (1809–1865) The 16th president was born in Kentucky and spent his early years in a variety of manual jobs in Ohio and Indiana. Lincoln was largely self-educated. He was interested in politics at an early age and ran for the House of Representatives in 1832 but lost. Lincoln, in addition to studying surveying, had been writing bills for the Whig party and acting as a lawyer in Illinois. A stint in the Illinois state legislature brought him face to face with Stephen Douglas, who defeated him in 1858 for a Senate seat. After writing more supporting speeches for Republicans, he ran for the presidency and became the first Republican to win that office. As president he dealt with the attempt of the Confederacy to split the Union; the Civil War resulted. He freed all the slaves in Confederate territories by signing the Emancipation Proclamation in 1863. In 1864 he won reelection, defeating the Democratic nominee, General McClellan. Lincoln was beginning to consider the problems of reconstruction when he was assassinated by John Wilkes Booth, an actor.

London, Jack (1876–1916) Born in San Francisco, London's early life was rough. His father, an astrologer, deserted his mother. In order to help the family survive, London swept floors in saloons, was a pin boy in a bowling alley, and did odd jobs until winning a writing contest at the age of sixteen. After one semester at the University of California at Berkeley, London left to try to support himself by writing. In 1897 he took off for the Klondike. His experiences there resulted in his first book, published by McClure and Phillips. London married Bess Maddern, ran for mayor of Oakland, but was defeated. In 1903 *The Call of the Wild* came out and proved a success. In 1904 London wrote *The Sea Wolf* and fell in love with Charmian Kittedge. He divorced his first wife and tried again to win the mayoralty of Oakland; he was again defeated. He wrote *White* Fang (1906) and *The Iron Heel* (1908). A man of boundless energy, he constructed a boat in which he intended to sail around the world—*The Snark.* After getting sick in the Solomon Islands, however, he returned to Sonoma Valley, California, where he built a ranch. He wrote the autobiographical *Martin Eden* (1909) and later *John Barleycorn* (1913), an autobiographical story about a man's struggle with alcoholism. His health deteriorated. Disenchanted with socialism, London died in 1916, possibly from a drug overdose.

Norris, Frank (1870–1902) Originally from Chicago, Norris moved to San Francisco when he was fourteen. His early ambition was to be an artist but he took to writing poetry at the University of California at Berkeley. After entering Harvard for a year, he came under the influence of Lewis Gates. While at Harvard, Norris worked on *McTeague,* one of the rare and perhaps unique pieces of literature composed in a writing course. Although it was unfinished by the time Norris graduated, he completed it in 1897 and it was published in 1899 to acclaim. For a while Norris worked as a reader for the publishing firm of Doubleday, where he was responsible for the appearance in print of Dreiser's *Sister Carrie.* Norris wrote *The Pit* (1903), the second of his "Wheat trilogy" novels, and in 1900 his greatest work, *The Octopus.* He died at the age of 32 from untreated appendicitis.

Roosevelt, Theodore (1858–1919) The 26th president was a contrast to Abraham Lincoln. Roosevelt was born into a wealthy family but was sickly as a child, a trait that he tried to overcome through force of will—and strenuous activity—in cattle driving and big game hunting. The Spanish American War of 1898 brought him national attention with his famous charge up San Juan Hill. Becoming the youngest president ever on the assassination of William McKinley, Roosevelt brought a new vigor to the office. He believed that the office should be used to resolve conflicts between competing economic forces in America. Under his stewardship, large companies were broken up so that smaller ones had the chance to compete in the marketplace. The Sherman Anti-Trust Act broke up a railroad monopoly in the Northwest. He was an ardent conservationist and put thousands of acres aside for public use. He ensured the construction of the Panama Canal.

Stowe, Harriet Beecher (1811–1896) Stowe's father, Lyman Beecher, was the best-known evangelist of his time and he influenced his daughter profoundly. One of his sermons caused her to experience a religious rebirth at the age of fourteen and at twenty-five she married a professor of biblical literature. Her early experiences with servants and her early background gave her abolitionist sympathies, and from her mid-thirties on she was writing about the abolitionist cause. In 1850 the passage of the Fugitive Slave Act and her reading the novels of Sir Walter Scott impelled her to produce her first novel, *Uncle Tom's Cabin* (1852). The success of this book caused her to write *A Key to Uncle Tom's Cabin,* which explained the factual basis of the novel, derived largely from newspaper advertisements in *American Slavery as It Is* by Theodore Weld (1839). Her later fiction, *The Minister's Wooing* (1859) and *Oldtown Folks* (1869) followed. She died an honored, even revered, figure at 85 in her native New England.

Tubman, Harriet (1822–1913) Escaped slave and abolitionist. Harriet Tubman was born Araminta Ross in 1822 in Dorchester County, Maryland. Her life as a slave was filled with pain, humiliation, and hard labor. As an adolescent, she was struck in the head by a two-pound iron weight thrown by an overseer, and for the rest of her life suffered headaches, seizures, and even visions. Still bleeding from her injury, Tubman was sent back into the fields to work. In about 1844, Tubman married a free black man named John Tubman. At that time, she changed her name to Harriet. In 1849, slated to be sold away from her home and family, Tubman escaped to Philadelphia. Rather than luxuriating in her new found freedom, Tubman returned to Maryland to rescue her family and others. She was nicknamed "Moses" for her work in bringing dozens of slaves into freedom. During the Civil War (1861–1865), Tubman worked first as a cook and a nurse. Later, she served as a scout and a spy and even conducted a raid that freed more than 700 slaves. After the war, she was active in the woman suffrage movement. In 1869, she married a Civil War veteran named Nelson Davis, and the couple adopted a baby in 1874. She died in New York in 1913.

Twain, Mark See Clemens, Samuel Langhorne.

Wharton, Edith, née Jones (1862–1937) Edith Wharton was brought up to lead precisely the kind of life she came to despise. Her family was wealthy and, although as a child Wharton preferred reading—"a secret ecstasy of communication"—to socializing, she eventually married a friend of her brother, Teddy Wharton, whom she met in the fashionable resort of Bar Harbor, Maine. She began publishing stories and poems. She inherited a fortune for those times and went through an emotionally draining period, all the while continuing to write. Scribner's and Sons published several books, including a short story collection and a work on decorating houses, which sold well. She established a friendship with Henry James. Her husband took trips without Wharton, and she worked on her first big success *The House of Mirth* (1905). In 1906 she visited Paris, and eventually came to live in France. In 1908 Wharton had an affair with her close friend Morton Fullerton; she and Teddy divorced in 1913. Meanwhile, she wrote the works that have kept her name alive: *Madame de Treymes* (1907), *Ethan Frome* (1911), and *The Custom of the Country*. During World War I, she helped care for orphans and sick children. Devastated by the loss of her friend Henry James ("his friendship was the pride and honor of my life"), she established herself in Hyéres, France, where she composed her final masterpiece, *The Age of Innocence* (1920). Although many books followed, none had the force and impact of her earlier work. She succumbed to a stroke, a wealthy woman made even more so by her writings, in 1937.

Wheeler, John Hill (1806–1882) The purported owner of the slave Hannah Crafts. Wheeler was born into privilege in 1806 in Murfreesboro, North Carolina. He was educated at the Hertford Academy in Murfreesboro, where his classmates included a future U.S. senator and a North Carolina chief justice. In 1827, at the age of 21, he was elected to the North Carolina House of Commons, becoming the youngest member of the body. He was reelected to serve in the House of Commons twice, once in 1828 and again in 1829. Wheeler married Mary Elizabeth Brown in 1830, a woman who was, by all accounts, one of the best-educated women in the country at the time. Wheeler and his new wife were in Murfreesboro in August 1831 during the abortive slave uprising led by Nat Turner, in which Wheeler raised a group of volunteers to combat the uprising. During the next several years, Wheeler lost his wife, his father, and two of his three children. In 1837, Wheeler remarried to Ellen Oldmixon Sully (the Mrs. Wheeler of *The Bondwoman's Narrative*). Wheeler held several government appointments in Franklin Pierce's administration, including that of ambassador to

Nicaragua. He was home on leave from Nicaragua when his slave, Jane Johnson, was taken and freed by abolitionist Passmore Williamson. He died in 1882 and was buried in Georgetown.

Whitman, Walt (1819–1892) American poet, author of *Leaves of Grass*. Walt Whitman, among the greatest and most influential American poets, was born in Long Island, New York, the son of Walter Whitman, a Quaker carpenter, and Louisa Van Velsor, who was of Dutch extraction. Whitman was largely self-educated, and his reading included the Bible, Shakespeare, Dante, Homer, Goethe, Carlyle, and Emerson. When he was twelve years old, Whitman left school to be apprenticed to a printer, and he spent much of his adult life working in the printing and publishing industry, as a printer, writer, editor, and founder of two newspapers. In 1855 Whitman published the first edition of *Leaves of Grass*, a collection of twelve poems that Whitman expanded to thirty-three in 1856 and later revised and reissued several times. Whitman's use of free verse, his celebration of the glory of the common person, his use of a truly American language, and his candor about sexuality were all revolutionary and have influenced generations of poets worldwide. During the Civil War, Whitman lived in Washington, D.C., where he worked as a government clerk and nursed wounded soldiers in area hospitals, often using his meager salary to buy medical supplies for his patients. After the war, Whitman moved to Camden, New Jersey, in order to be near his dying mother. Although he suffered a paralytic stroke in 1873, Whitman continued to write and revise his poetry. The 1882 edition of *Leaves of Grass* was profitable enough that the proceeds allowed him to purchase a house in Camden, where he lived until his death in 1892.

Whittier, John Greenleaf (1807–1892) Poet and abolitionist. Whittier was born in 1807 in Haverhill, Massachusetts, into a family of staunch Quakers. As a boy, Whittier was sickly and could not provide much help in working the family farm. He loved to read, however, and immersed himself in his father's half dozen books about Quakerism. He began writing poetry at an early age. He was first published in 1826 when his sister sent a poem, "The Exile's Departure," to the *Newburyport Free Press*. The editor of the Free Press, abolitionist William Lloyd Garrison, persuaded Whittier to attend the newly opened Haverhill Academy. Money was scarce, and Whittier worked as a shoemaker and teacher to pay his tuition. He completed his entire high-school education in two terms. Whittier worked as an editor and writer for newspapers for several years. In 1833, he published an antislavery pamphlet entitled *Justice and Expediency* and helped to found the American Anti-Slavery Society. From 1835 to 1838, Whittier traveled widely, lobbying and speaking on behalf of the abolitionist cause. He was often stoned and run out of town by pro-slavery mobs. In 1839, Wittier helped to found the Liberty Party, which he hoped would help change the attitude of the public about slavery. In about 1845, Whittier had a breakdown and returned to Amesbury, Massachusetts, where he lived for the rest of his life. He continued to advocate abolitionist causes. Before the Civil War (1861–1865), Whittier's had published two volumes of antislavery poetry. After the war, he changed his focus and in 1866 published his most famous work, *Snow Bound*. Whittier died in 1892.

Williamson, Passmore (1820–1895) Abolitionist who challenged the Fugitive Slave Act of 1850. Williamson, a Quaker, was born in Wettstown, Pennsylvania, in 1822. In July of 1855, Williamson was working for the Pennsylvania Anti-Slavery Society. The society had received word that Jane Johnson, an enslaved person belonging to John Hill Wheeler, wanted freedom for herself and her two sons. Williamson caught up with Wheeler's party on board a steamer just as they were leaving Philadelphia. "You are the person I am looking for, I presume," Williamson said to Johnson. Before she could answer, Wheeler demanded to know what he wanted. "Nothing," said Williamson. His business was "entirely with this woman." "She is my slave," Wheeler replied, "and anything you have to say to her you can say to me." "You may have been his slave," said Williamson to Johnson, "but you are now free." Johnson escaped, and Williamson was later convicted of contempt of court and served a brief sentence in Moyamensing Prison. While he was in prison, Williamson became a cause célèbre for abolitionists everywhere. Williamson died in 1895.

Further Reading

Chapter 1. Sectionalism, Industrialism, and Literary Regionalism

Berthoff, Warner. *The Ferment of Realism: American Literature, 1884-1919.* New York: Free Press, 1965.

Borus, Daniel H. *Writing Realism: Howells, James, and Norris in the Mass Market.* Chapel Hill: University of North Carolina Press, 1989.

Foote, Stephanie. *Regional Fictions: Culture and Identity in Nineteenth-Century American Literature.* Madison: University of Wisconsin Press, 2001.

Minter, David. *A Cultural History of the American Novel: Henry James to William Faulkner.* New York: Cambridge University Press, 1994.

Nettels, Elsa. *Language and Gender in American Fiction: Howells, James, Wharton, and Cather.* Charlottesville: University of Virginia Press, 1997.

Warren, Kenneth W. *Black and White Strangers: Race and American Literary Realism.* Chicago: University of Chicago Press, 1993.

Weber, Ronald. *The Midwestern Ascendancy in American Writing.* Bloomington: Indiana University Press, 1992.

Chapter 2. Slave Narratives and Race Relations

Foster, Francis Smith. *Witnessing History.* Second edition. Madison: University of Wisconsin Press, 1993.

Gossett, Thomas F. *Uncle Tom's Cabin and American Culture.* Dallas: Southern Methodist University Press, 1985.

Greenblatt, Stephen. *Marvellous Possessions: The Wonder of the New World.* Chicago: University of Chicago Press, 1992.

Spelman, Elizabeth V. *Fruits of Sorrow: Framing Our Attention to Suffering.* Boston: Beacon Press, 1997.

Trafton, Scott. *Egypt Land: Race and Nineteenth Century America.* Durham: Duke University Press, 2004.

Chapter 3. Mark Twain

Chase, Richard. *The American Novel and Its Tradition.* New York: Gordian Press, 1957.

Cox, James. *Mark Twain: The Fate of Humor.* Princeton: Princeton University Press, 1966.

Fiedler, Leslie. *Love and Death in the American Novel.* New York: Stein and Day, 1966.

Fishkin: Shelley Fisher. *Was Huck Black?* New York: Oxford University Press, 1993.

Skaggs, H. M. *The Folk of Southern Fiction.* Athens: University of Georgia Press, 1972.

Wallace, John H. *"The Case against Huck Finn."* In James S. Leonard et al., eds. *Satire or Evasion: The Case against "Huckleberry Finn."* Durham: Duke University Press, 1992.

Chapter 4. Urban Novels and Internationalism

Kazin, Alfred. *On Native Grounds.* New York: Reynal and Hitchock, 1942.

Bell, Michael Davitt. *The Problem of Realism: Studies in the Cultural History of a Literary Idea.* Chicago: University of Chicago Press, 1993.

Brodhead, Richard. *Cultures of Letters: Scenes of Reading and Writing in Nineteenth-Century American Literature.* Chicago: University of Chicago Press, 1995.

Cady, Edwin H. *The Light of Common Day: Realism in American Fiction.* Bloomington: Indiana University Press, 1971.

[James, Henry] http://www2.newpaltz.edu/~hathaway

Chapter 5. Regionalism

Knight, Grant C. *The Critical Period in American Literature.* Chapel Hill: University of North Carolina Press, 1951.

Lynn, Kenneth S. *Mark Twain and South Western Humor.* Westport, CT: Greenwood, 1972.

Taylor, Walter Fuller. *The Economic Novel in America.* Chapel Hill: University of North Carolina, Press, 1942.

Wilson, Edmund. *Patriotic Gore.* New York: Oxford University Press, 1962.

http://guweb2gonza.edu/faculty/campbell/en1311.regbib.htm

Chapter 6. Naturalism, Determinism, and Social Reform

Cook, Fred J. *The Muckrakers: Crusading Journalists Who Changed America.* New York: Doubleday, 1972.

Homberger, Eric. *American Writers and Radical Politics, 1900–39.* New York: St. Martin's Press, 1986.

Irving, Katrina. *Immigrant Mothers.* Urbana: University of Illinois Press, 2000.

Rideout, Walter. *The Radical Novel in the United States 1900–1954.* Cambridge: Harvard University Press, 1956.

Ziff, Larzer. *The American 1890's: Life and Times of a Lost Generation.* New York: Viking Press, 1966.

Chapter 7. Other African American Voices

Crafts, Hannah. *The Bondswoman's Narrative.* New York: Warner, 2002.

Gates, Henry Louis. *The Signifying Monkey: A Theory of African American Literary Criticism.* New York: Oxford University Press, 1989.

Gates, Henry Louis, Jr., and Hollis Robbins, eds. *In Search of Hannah Crafts: Critical Essays on* The Bondwoman's Narrative. New York: Basic Civitas Books, 2004.

Ward, Andrew. *The Slaves's War: The Civil War in the Words of Former Slaves.* New York: Houghton Mifflin, 2008.

Wilson, Harriet. *Our Nig: Sketches from the Life of a Free Black.* New York: Dover, 2005.

Index